To our
Congressman Thomas R. Carper
1987

Charles a

3.00

Pills, Pen & Politics

A Biography of Leon Jastremski

Leon Jastremski, from the Edward Lis portrait owned by the Captain Stanislaus Mlotkowski Memorial Bridgade Society and on exhibit in the Polish Memorial Room, Fort Delaware. (Presented by the members of the Jastremski Family)

PILLS, PEN & POLITICS

The Story of General Leon Jastremski 1843-1907

by Edward Pinkowski

Captain Stanislaus Mlotkowski Memorial Brigade Society
247 Philadelphia Pike
Wilmington, Delaware 19809

Copyright 1974 by
Edward Pinkowski
All rights reserved

Library of Congress Catalog Card Number 74-29094
ISBN 0-9600814-1-0

Printed in the United States of America

TO HELEN AND BETTY

WHOSE HUSBANDS

CHARLES KILCZEWSKI AND EDWARD SKOMORUCHA

INVOLVED THEM IN THIS BOOK

Other Books by

EDWARD PINKOWSKI

Lattimer Massacre

History of Bridgeport, Pa.

Washington's Officers Slept Here

Forgotten Fathers

Chester County Place Names

John Siney—The Miners' Martyr

Anthony Sadowski—Polish Pioneer

Table of Contents

Frontispiece

Preface 9

1. Seeds of Glory 15
2. Uprooted Lives 23
3. The Big Soldier 35
4. Prisoner of War 49
5. Ordeal of Fire and Starvation 65
6. Proud Cavalier of Louisiana 83
7. Consul in Callao 99
8. The Last Campaign 115

Appendices:
   1. Descendants of Leon Jastremski 124
   2. Selected Letters 125
   3. Platform of Gen. Jastremski for governor in 1903 133
   4. Gen. Jastremski's Position on Labor 141
   5. Votes for Governor of Louisiana in Primary Election, Jan. 19, 1904 145
   6. Gen. Jastremski's Platform for governor in 1907 147

Bibliographical Notes 152

Index 167

Illustrations .... Between pages 81 and 83

Preface

> I hain't forgot my raisin',
>   Nor how, in sixty two
> Or thereabouts, with battle shouts,
>   I charged the boys in blue;
> And I say I fought with Stonewall
>   And blazed the way with Lee,
> But if this old Union's in for war
>   Make one more gun for me!

THUS, in New Orleans on the morning of April 2, 1898, Leon Jastremski, a self-made Julius Caesar who, at the age of fifty-four, filled every position he ever held with credit to himself, read from a newspaper clipping on his desk at 2003 Carondelet Street. The poem, "Make One More Gun For Me!" epitomized his feelings in the midst of a public outcry for Spain to get out of Cuba on account of sinking the U. S. battleship *Maine*. As he sat in front of a typewriter, composing a letter to William McKinley, President of the United States, the memories came flooding back: of his enlisting as a private in the 10th Louisiana Infantry when he was a mere lad and following the flag of Jefferson Davis and the Confederacy; of his promotions to Sergeant Major, First Lieutenant and Captain before he was nineteen years old; of his participation in the bloody campaigns of the Army of Northern Virginia from the lines of Yorktown to the "bloody angle" at Spottsylvania, where he was captured for the third time in the war; of his ordeal with 600 Confederate officers under fire on Morris Island, starvation on a prison ship, and of his escape when he was being taken back to Fort Delaware.

He would tell the President of his appointments by two governors as Brigadier General in the Louisiana National Guard, of his knowledge of French and Spanish, of his powers of endurance, and of the four years he spent as United States consul at Callao, Peru. He began the letter as follows:

"I have the honor hereby, in the event of war, to tender to you my services to aid in upholding the national flag."

The 25-line letter, delivered to President McKinley in Washington, D. C., by Louisiana's senior senator, Donelson Caffery, mirrored, to a small extent, the tortuous course of human events in Leon Jastremski's life. This is not a definitive study of those events. It is also not an exhaustive study of the ambitions, pulsations, victories, defeats, loves, hatreds, and achievements that shaped his career.

This is a story—not a definitive biography—of a Polish-Franco-American. Until 1861 the story of his life is as faint as the crumbling, lichened characters on his gravestone in Baton Rouge. Too young to be brought over to Louisiana at the time his parents came, a short time after his birth in 1843, he grew to the age of six years with his mother's relatives in a mountain village of southern France and was sent off to Vermilionville, now known as Lafayette, Louisiana, where his father, a Polish exile, was a medical doctor. Four years later the family moved to Abbeville, not far away, where Leon Jastremski was left an orphan at the age of fourteen, and at that early age became the architect of his own fortune.

Into the panorama of his life there are woven many pictures. From a printer's devil and drugstore clerk he became a Confederate soldier. From President Lincoln's standpoint, he was mistaken; from his, he was a patriot. Through four years of weary marching, attacks and repulses, victories and defeats, hardships, and untold privations, he espoused the Southern cause and performed well the duties of a soldier. Had he not been captured three times, and confined in military prisons, there can be little doubt that he would have earned and achieved higher rank than captain.

In camp, on the march, in battle and in prison he learned lessons more difficult than those taught in schools. He escaped from a prison ship and returned to a land torn apart by war, its plantations in ruins, its educational institutions closed, many of its young men buried on battlefields, and gloom hanging like a sombre pall over the whole land.

Rising from this 19th century Valhalla, without the advantages of wealth, education, or family influence, he gained a niche in American history through the force of his own ability, character, and efforts. His public service spanned the administrations of six governors, eight presidents, and five decades of American history. One finds him moving majestically across the pages of almost every Louisiana newspaper almost from the time he took off his Civil War uniform to his death in 1907.

He lived to see the plantations of Louisiana rise again. He lived to see the sails of commerce whiten the waterways around him. He lived to see his own State one of the leaders in the manufacture of rice and sugar. He lived to see the colleges and universities spring up anew where they had been paralyzed or destroyed by war. He lived to help return the ballot to his comrades in arms from whom it had been taken, and he lived to resist Federal interference with local and State elections. He did not believe a candidate should be forced upon the voters, whether they liked him or not, and campaigned twice as a gubernatorial candidate largely on the issue of primary elections in Louisiana.

Nothing would have delighted him more than the knowledge that, nearly seven decades after his death, he still created interest in his life. Could his wish be known, it would probably be that his life, like the face of Oliver Cromwell, should be represented just as it was. It is related that when Peter Lelvy, a famous portrait painter, suggested to Cromwell that he would eliminate from the painting a mole on his face, Cromwell replied: "I desire you would use all your skill to paint my picture truly like me, and not flatter me at all; keep all these roughnesses, pimples, warts, and everything as you see me, otherwise I will never pay a farthing for it." Could Leon Jastremski's wish be known, it would be that his life, like the face of Cromwell, should be represented just as it was.

All that the present volume claims to be is a preliminary look at Leon Jastremski, not at the world he represented, and deals with many activities only in so far as they influenced him. It, therefore, passes very lightly over his contributions to the growth and development of Baton Rouge, his journalistic career, his work in the Democratic party, and his campaigns for governor of Louisiana, which ought to be the objects of special study; it only looks at them in a way to understand his part in the drama of American culture.

In the research, writing, and publication of this book, I am indebted to many persons who have given generously of their time, labor, money, and advice. First of all, to Leon Jastremski's granddaughter, Mrs. Sarah Land Jastremski Helm, who patiently suffered my intrusions while she tried to entertain her grandchildren and lent me all the material I asked for, and to George Reymond, the patriarch of the Jastremski family and grandnephew of Leon Jastremski, who guided me to the uncatalogued family papers, scrapbooks, and photographs in the possession of various members of the clan. Laura Reymond was also of great service. Only a few relatives and, until my visit to Mrs. Helm's home in New Iberia, Louisiana, no historian had seen the letters Leon Jastremski wrote during the Civil War. But, as everyone will realize, Mrs. Helm provided me with a gold mine of material to write a much longer book, had time been available, without troubling the other descendants of Dr. Vincent Jastremski for odd items of information to piece out an interesting biography. A thousand kisses to her!

I am most grateful to Helen and Charles Kilczewski who guided me, encouraged me, helped me, comforted me, and goaded me all along the way.

My greatest debt, beyond describing, is to my wife, Connie.

I gratefully acknowledge my indebtedness to all of the previous writers of articles or columns on General Jastremski. Also, for permitting me to examine and quote from diaries and manuscripts in their custody, I wish to thank each of the following: Miss Eleanor S. Brockenbrough, Librarian, The Museum of the Confederacy, Richmond, Va.; Miss Joyce Amedee, Catholic Life Center, Baton Rouge, La.; the Rare Book Room, Library of Congress, and War Records Division, National Archives, Washington, D. C.; Louisiana State University, Baton Rouge, La., and Historical Society of Pennsylvania, Philadelphia.

I am also indebted to the library staffs in Philadelphia, New Orleans, Baton Rouge, Lafayette, Abbeville, and to the following persons: Mrs. Harriet Callahan, Patrick Darcy, Thomas J. Baker, Jr., Ernest Gueymard, Ms. Moreen Kattie, Walter Staszczak, Martin Cupery, W. Emerson Wilson, Mrs. Lillian Steen Derveloy, Mr. and Mrs. Albert Steen, and many others.

For the church records in their custody, I am indebted to Rev. Msgr. Richard von Phul Mouton, pastor, St. Mary Magdalen, Abbeville, and Rev. Msgr. George A. Bodin, pastor, St. John's Cathedral, Lafayette, Louisiana. Also, Ralph R. Bienvenu, publisher of *Abbeville Meridional*.

Whenever I visit the National Archives for historical research, there are always familiar faces to whom I turn for assistance. Among those who located Jastremski material for me were Michael P. Musick, Del Floyd, James Stewart, James Walker, and Albert Blair. Thanks, archivists!

A different order of gratitude is owed to Henry Archacki upon whom I imposed a special friendship tax.

Finally, I wish to express my gratitude to the officers and members of the Captain Stanislaus Mlotkowski Memorial Brigade Society for supplying me with their monogrammed pens and encouraging me to use them until this work was done.

EDWARD PINKOWSKI

Philadelphia, Pa.
October 10, 1974

1

Seeds of Glory

BEFORE Leon Jastremski and I were cast together in this labor of love, two persons I first met in Fort Delaware on June 27, 1965, gave me differing impressions of the Polish-Franco-American who was recognized years ago throughout Louisiana as a "man of sterling qualities, of eminent ability, of great force of character, of large experience in public affairs and the soul of honor and truth."[1] We were in a large suite, partly filled with the paraphernalia of a Civil War mess hall and kitchen and objects of interest that held visitors in noble bondage with Polish participants in the saga of Fort Delaware, and one of the exhibits which attracted me like a magnet was a tableau of General Jastremski.[2]

Under a heading, "Captain Jastremski was the South's most famous Polish prisoner at Fort Delaware," Henry Archacki, a Polish born artist and lover of Polish historical subjects, created a story of Jastremski in pictures. He portrayed him as a printer's devil at the age of fourteen when he had to get on a soap box in order to reach the typesetter's case and set type, in English and in French, for a bilingual weekly newspaper in Abbeville, Louisiana. He profiled him as a stripling youth, a Confederate captain of handsome form and gallant mien, but spirited as a cavalier, who offered himself for slaughter. The people of Baton Rouge elected him mayor of their city in 1876, as shown in a third panel, and, among other achievements, he returned the Louisiana seat of government to Baton Rouge. It's still there! The fourth corner of the Archacki masterpiece gave any viewer whose name ended in "ski" a feeling that his name was not a barrier to success, for Jastremski ran twice for governor of Louisiana but death cheated him of a lifelong ambition.

Sigmund Uminski, author of almost a dozen books on Polish subjects, gave me a different impression of the Confederate officer from Louisiana. After spending several weeks in the archives of the Pelican State, he put his findings together in a lecture he gave to members of the Polish American Historical Association in 1964 and in articles he wrote for a number of periodicals.³ Archacki took what he wrote about Jastremski in the now-defunct *American Polonia Reporter* and combined it with his art work. The reproduction, small but well-designed, was hung on the wall of the large room in which I met Archacki and Uminski.

To most Americans this was all that they knew about Leon Jastremski. But neither Archacki nor Uminski prepared me for the development of a positive ethnic consciousness that I observed in the small but active group that conducted Polish memorial events on Pea Patch Island. It seems more relevant today than it seemed when I first became aware of it. It is relevant because, more clearly than at any other time in the nation's history, the officers and members of the Captain Stanislaus Mlotkowski Memorial Brigade Society are a shining example of ethnicity in American life and deserve a separate chapter in the story of Leon Jastremski.

Until 1965 Jastremski was virtually in oblivion. Like Pulaski and Kosciuszko, he was a notable figure in the American past, but, unlike the two Polish heroes of the American Revolution, historians and biographers have paid little attention to him. They have naturally found it easier to write about diarists and letter writers, the financial tycoons, railroad kings, and industrial moguls, the indiscreet men who left juicy stories of their actions in the newspapers. When Jastremski is mentioned at all in histories of Louisiana, he appears only incidentally as a foil for some governor or as an officer in some organization. Biographers apparently did not think of him as a living, breathing human being—with all the compounded virtues and vices that go to make up a notable American.

But the officers and members of the Fort Delaware brigade, largely made up of Polish immigrants and their American-born children, looked at Jastremski quite differently. They learned from commemorating past transients of the island, whether they belonged to the garrison during the Civil War or to the prison population, that every man's life, in a narrower or wider sense, is an ideal for other men. Whether it be lowly or exalted, whether it be humble or great, there is among every man's associates some person who will look to him as a model of his own conduct, who will find in him something worthy of imitation, and who will dis-cover for himself and feel for himself that he is somebody. Showing pride in a man with a Polish name created self-esteem in persons who in the past often were told to change their names, adopt American manners and customs, and assume a common but stereotype role in society.

Before the majority of scholars, musicians, teachers, artists, legislators, television producers, radio programmers and others jumped on the bandwagon to deal with ethnic themes, the leaders of the Polish community in Wilmington, Delaware, were doing something to perpetuate their heritage. Among them was Vincent J. Kowalewski, a thoughtful and articulate man in his fifties, an insurance agent, conductor of a Polish radio program, and secretary of the Council of Polish Societies and Clubs in Delaware. Prior to the Second World War he edited and published a Polish language newspaper, *Wiadomosci,* which kept his subscribers abreast of the times. He exercised a marked influence upon the cultural life of Polish settlers in the Wilmington area.

On September 25, 1958, W. Emerson Wilson, a neat, well-dressed newspaperman, wrote to him that the Fort Delaware Society, which he headed, was unable to restore the whole interior of the old fort on Pea Patch Island and invited the 15-year-old Polish council to restore one of the rooms in memory of Captain Stanislaus Mlotkowski, a native of Poland who commanded a Union artillery company at the fort during the Civil War. He noted that he had a photograph of Captain Mlotkowski and offered to show it to the Polish group.[4]

Wilson's proposal fell into the right hands. "So far as I can see," Kowalewski said to his closest friends, "the Poles of Wilmington need something to keep them alive and perpetuate their culture. I think this is a good suggestion. Let's act positively on it."

Kowalewski replied to Wilson on October first and suggested that someone come to the next meeting of the executive board of the Polish council to discuss the proposal in more detail.[5] The meeting was held on Tuesday evening, October 28, in the Polish American Civic Association, 618 South Franklin Street, Wilmington, and William P. Frank, historian of the Fort Delaware Society, spent some time exchanging ideas with Kowalewski and other board members and encouraging them to restore one of the rooms of Fort Delaware for tourists during the Civil War centennial.

As a result, eight persons were picked by the Polish council to visit Fort Delaware and select a room for restoration. They included Helen Kilczewski, a tall, beautiful woman who devoted most of her energy to Polish American cultural affairs, Frank J. Leski, a real estate dealer, Czeslawa Klaczkiewicz, one of the founders of the Polish War Mothers in Wilmington, Ludwig Kopec, a chemical engineer, Joseph Strzalkowski, Joseph Falkowski, and Bronislawa Stepnowski, three energetic supporters of the fight for Poland's independence, and Kowalewski. None of them had previously been to Fort Delaware.[6]

Wilson made arrangements to meet the eight delegates on Saturday afternoon, November 22, in a waterfront tavern at Delaware City, twelve miles south of Wilmington, and to have Captain Walter Wisowaty's boat ready to take them to the island in the middle of the Delaware River. The day was damp and cold. Mrs. Kilczewski took three or four delegates in her car, and Kowalewski took the others. They arrived in Captain Wisowaty's tavern half-frozen, and Wilson and his wife immediately led them to a bar on which the Polish tavern keeper and boat captain had set delicious snacks and warm drinks. The reception fortified them for an inspection of the cold rooms inside the fort.

They were able to see only the rooms on the first floor of the two buildings which were used by the garrison during the Civil War. The iron stairways to the upper floors were gone. Most of them had been taken by vandals and sold for scrap between 1945 and 1951 when the fort and the island became a state historical park. The rooms were in awful condition. The delegates were almost discouraged. What could they do with stripped and mutilated rooms? When Mrs. Kilczewski suggested that the group take what was formerly the enlisted men's mess hall and kitchen, Wilson shook his head. The suite of rooms needed windows, doors, and other repairs. He thought the group could not raise enough money to restore the rooms. But Mrs. Kilczewski realized that when the rooms were eventually opened to the public they could lock the two doors leading to them from the parade ground without having people go through them to reach other parts of the buildings.

No steps were taken to do any work in the rooms until delegates of the Polish council met in January, 1959, and chose Edward Skomorucha, a young television serviceman and salesman with an attractive wife and three bright children, to deal with the problems of restoration, memorabilia, and maintenance of the Polish memorial.[7] He was selected because of his ability to promote a project and to get along with juxtaposed elements in the Polish community more or less at odds with one another. He was 43 years old and, at six foot one and 185 pounds, a picture of finely conditioned physical power. He had the good will of the Polish people and the enthusiasm to turn the dream of a fitting memorial to Polish defenders of America to reality.

Charles Kilczewski, whom he met at a dance in St. Stanislaus parish hall in Wilmington's East Side many years ago, described how Skomorucha set the stage for the monumental work. The Fort Delaware committee had only forty-seven dollars in the bank when the two exchanged words on the cost of installing new windows and doors, repairing and cleaning the brick walls, and other work. Having been in brick restoration work at least fifteen years, and having experienced pointers, plasterers and bricklayers who had worked for his father-in-law for years prior to his joining the John Palczewski firm, Kilczewski replied: "Ed, you've come forward with a whole lot of ideas, but this is undoubtedly the costliest one."[8]

"How much will it cost to do the work?" Skomorucha asked.

"Five thousand dollars," Kilczewski replied, but Skomorucha was not to be deterred from his purpose. He had decided, no matter what happened to him or how much money was in the bank, to plunge into the Fort Delaware project.

"Go ahead and do the work," he told Kilczewski. "I'll worry about the money."

As a result of Skomorucha's courage, everybody began to stir, to change positions, like leaves suddenly lifted in a breeze. Enthusiasm grew. The grind was too much for some of the delegates who made the first visit to the fort, and as they dropped out, other members of the Polish community, younger, prettier, and livelier, took their places. "The man who showed the most interest was Vincent Kowalewski," Helen Kilczewski recalled. "He pushed the memorial room on his radio program, and when he died, his widow, Josephine, for a year or so, and then Joe Dabrowski picked up where he left off. From the start, John Kowalewski typed letters for his father, and Joanne, Vince's daughter, now Mrs. Magdycz, was active with me and other women in bingo parties and other fund-raising activities. Among them were Ann and Blanche Stepnowski, Aniela Turochy, Julia Baczkowski, Adela Babiarz, Jean Paruszewski, Tillie Blozis, Caroline Kucharska, and many others. I'm sorry I cannot remember them all."[9]

Other friendships proliferated. The names of the early male members of the Fort Delaware committee roll out—it is impossible to remember them all. Walter Staszczak left his photo shop to lend a hand, Walt Stan his artist's studio, Ben Pawlikowski and Anthony Liszkiewicz their butcher shops, Edward Garbowski his beloved Falsons, Edmund Dabrowski his church choir, Adam Rosiak his political post, John Babiarz the mayor's office in Wilmington, Wm. Czacharowski his florist shop, Casimir Jonkiert and John Yasik. The Sobocinski brothers, Zenon and Stanley, Charles L. Paruszewski, Esq., and Anthony Witt, were very helpful.

As soon as Kilczewski and his crew finished their work, the Fort Delaware committee dedicated the suite of rooms in memory of Captain Stanislaus Mlotkowski, a Polish immigrant from Philadelphia who had spent more time at Fort Delaware than any other Pole during the Civil War. Helen Kilczewski unveiled Walt Stan's portrait of the Polish artillery officer over the fireplace in the large, high-ceilinged room. The dedication took place a century, minus a day, after Mlotkowski was appointed First Lieutenant in the Independent Battery A, Pennsylvania Light Artillery. He was promoted to the rank of captain on March 1, 1862, and served at Fort Delaware throughout the war.

For the next twelve years, from 1961 on, while racial violence rose like a monster throughout the nation, the members of the Mlotkowski brigade went right on hosting their own brand of revolutionary change. They held a commemorative program each year that would grab the largest possible audience. It would be hard to find a more picturesque and stimulating series of activities than those the brigade conducted inside the fort. The sound of Polish liturgy, filling the ear for a moment, lingering transiently in echo from the brick-arched casements of the fort, the smell of Polish cooking, the sight of polka dancers on a small wooden platform, the words of praise of Captain Mlotkowski, General Schoepf, Colonel Karge, and other contributors to America's strength, the children's games and the memorabilia in the Polish shrine—all filled the ears, eyes, and brains of the spectators and flowed through their hearts like maddening wine.

The longer the brigade exists, the more it learns about various lesser historical figures who had been brushed aside in the past by the worship of Pulaski, Kosciuszko, and the Jamestown Poles. It has unrolled the records of the principal Polish notables in the past of Fort Delaware, and new seeds of glory wait to spring from untapped archives. John Kowalewski, who served as master of ceremonies almost every year during the 1960's, once told me, "We have a lot of ethnic heroes to go."

Naturally, every ethnic group should enshrine its own heroes. But few ethnic groups do it the way the Mlotkowski brigade does. The members of the brigade have learned how to realize their conceptions, understand the social meaning of their work, and gain from celebrating past events and human beings a new sense of dedication. They know that remembrances of their forebears, even if they were very difficult at times, are for every American of Polish descent a pure and bright page of his life. Not all Poles have this awareness.

Early in 1974, the group, under the chairmanship of Benjamin S. Yatkowski, Sr., and supported by such newer members as Florence Nowak (1965), Josephine Reimer, the Kozlowskis, Janina and Walter Maczynski (1963), the Palczewskis, Frank Plitt, Emilie Kozinski, the Rybaltowskis, the Smulskis, the Terepkas, Julianna Kilczewski Tice (1965) and her children, the Norths, the Tomczyks, and Raymond Babiarz, chose General Leon Jastremski to memorialize on June ninth at Fort Delaware, where he was a prisoner of war in 1862-64, and sent Charles Kilczewski to Baton Rouge, Louisiana, for pictures of General Jastremski's grave, visits with members of the Jastremski family, and a selection of Jastremski memorabilia for exhibition in the Polish memorial room of Fort Delaware.[10]

The General's grandnephew, George H. Reymond, and his wife, Laura, visited Fort Delaware on June ninth, and they have a mental picture of the first part of the program as clear as a steel engraving.[11] At the opening of a Catholic Mass on the edge of the parade ground, just in front of the Polish memorial, Walter Staszczak, dressed as if he were Captain Stanislaus Mlotkowski, walked to the center of the altar from the left, and Stanley Sobocinski, posing as Captain Leon Jastremski in a Confederate gray uniform, came from the right. The two shook hands in the sign of peace in front of the altar and each one stepped to the rear of the side from which he came, one representing the North and the other the South, and remained at attention throughout the Sunday mass.[12]

Like a flash of light there passed through Reymond's mind the thought that the reincarnation of his granduncle had not only thus opened the way for him, but with an imperative finger had directed him to make a sacramental offering to the historical rites. When he returned to Louisiana, he talked to other members of the Jastremski family about putting the idea into concrete form and received their approval. He commissioned Edward Lis, an internationally known portrait artist from Gulph Mills, Pennsylvania, to paint an oil portrait of Leon Jastremski as a Confederate captain at the age of twenty, just as he possibly looked when he was a prisoner of war at Fort Delaware, and, symbolically, Sarah Jastremski Helm, like a good retriever, brought out of her trinket box a hardly visible image of her grandfather which was miraculously used for the portrait.

The presentation of Captain Jastremski's portrait to the Captain Stanislaus Mlotkowski Memorial Brigade Society is more than symbolic of the chain of history which links us together in the heritage of our forebears.[13] No, it is not a symbol, not a false object of note, but something far-reaching and impalpable, like the true expression of an emotion. As Theocritus said in the third century, "a great love goes here with a little gift," or as Joseph Conrad, the great Polish writer, wrote in the preface of *The Nigger of the Narcissus,* "a gift and not an acquisition—and, therefore, more permanently enduring."

2

Uprooted Lives

"It is the custom of all biographers," wrote the eighteenth century novelist and playwright, Henry Fielding, whose works Leon Jastremski collected for many years and then presented to an educational group in Louisiana, "at their entrance into their work, to step a little backwards and to trace up their hero, as the ancients did the river Nile, till an incapacity of proceeding higher puts an end to their search."[1]

The ancestral roots of Leon Jastremski, at least prior to 1735, are obscure. It is possible to find families of the same name, originally Jastrzebski, on the land between the Baltic Sea and the Black Sea, and, if we include other versions and variations of the name, the trail extends westward as far as France, Spain, Portugal, and even the British Isles. The Hawks of England are the Jastrzebskis of that country. In English, the name, freely translated, means hawk place, and is derived from the Polish word for hawk, *jastrzab*.

People named Jastrzebski have received brief notices in the written records of Poland since the Tatar invasion in the twelfth century. Agnes Jastrzebski, mother superior of a Franciscan convent in Zawichośc, sixty nuns, and thirteen priests were slain by Tatars while praying in a Catholic church in 1282. Nicholas and Stephen Jastrzebski, members of the Polish nobility in Gostyn, verified the election of King Wladyslaw IV in 1632. Another Jastrzebski, a Michael, took part in the election of John Sobieski, commander of the Polish army, as King John III in 1673.[2]

No province in Poland was without its share of Jastrzebskis, from Basil in Poznan, Dominick in Kujawy, Joseph and Benedict in Lukowsk to Thomas and Joseph Jastrzebski in Lithuania. John Jastrzebski was the king's steward of Lubelsk in 1489. The Polish ancestors of Leon Jastremski were rooted in the eastern borderlands of Poland, mostly in the provinces of Podolia and Kamieniec. King John Casimir lost the two provinces by the treaty of Buczazc in 1672. It could easily have been

Michael Jastrzebski who persuaded King John III to recover Podolia four years later.

The concern in this chapter is mainly with the Polish ancestors of Leon Jastremski. The other Jastrzebskis in Poland may not be related to him. The pattern of dispersal, however, almost coincides with the migrations of Sarmatians, a forgotten group of nomads in medieval times, and consequently it behooves us to consider the possibility that his forebears brought to Poland, or its counterpart, a millenium and a half ago the earliest farming techniques, new ways of breeding stock and making weapons, art, and religion. Unprotected by any natural barriers, the elements in this group, known as Alans, experienced many changes by the advances of Huns, Goths, and Tatars into their territory between the third and twelfth centuries. The close contacts which existed for the most part between the Sarmatians and other settlers, strengthened by intermarriage, ultimately resulted in the Polonization of the mixed population.[3]

Archaeological remains of the once powerful Sarmatians, such as stone slabs and iron spearheads with silver inlaid tamga signs, richly furnished graves, wheel-turned pottery, tendrilled brooches, belt buckles, and other ancient artifacts, have been found in the basin of the Upper Dniester River where the ancestors of Leon Jastremski lived. The root "Yas," either an element of Leon's surname or a corruption of Ptolemy's Asioi, after its exposure to Polish culture in the basin of the Upper Dniester, appeared in the names of many places, including the first capital of Moldavia, and was linked to tribes from Podolia and Kamieniec as early as the sixth century.[4]

"A belief in the Sarmatian origin of Poland was widespread for centuries among the Polish nobility," wrote Dr. Tadeusz Sulimirski, formerly Professor of Prehistoric Archaeology at the Jagiellonian University of Cracow. "Tamga signs appear on eleventh century coins, and the most striking survival is in Polish heraldry, where ancient tamgas appear in stylized form as crescents, arrows, horseshoes, etc."[5]

Little remains of Jastremski family records to remind the modern world of their early existence in the land of the white eagle. When Leon Jastremski's father, Vincent, received his medical degree from the French government on April 6, 1836, the date and birthplace were noted on the diploma, but not very clearly, and consequently the word, "probably," so far as the evidence shows, has to precede their use.[6] Two and a half years later Dr. Jastremski, or Yastrzemski as he sometimes wrote it, received a letter from his mother at Schtcherbowietz near Nowo Uschitzk in Kamienietz Podolski.[7] Combining the two records together, it is safe to assume that Vincent Jastremski was born there on the first day of November in 1806.

The province in which he was born was since the partition of Poland in 1796 under the rule of two Russian czars. Czar Alexander I mounted the throne in 1801 over the body of his murdered father, Paul I, and was chiefly remembered for a melancholic life of unfulfilled promises and for making his younger brother, Constantine, head of the army in the Russian provinces that had formerly belonged to the kingdom of Poland. On the death of Alexander in 1825, his youngest brother, Nicholas, after Constantine renounced the throne, inherited the corrupt and police-ridden Russian empire.

The Polish masses didn't like either brother, and on the evening of November 29, 1830, Piotr Wysocki,[8] an impoverished, 33-year-old nobleman from Warka and drill instructor of the Warsaw Military Academy, called upon his loyal cadets to turn against the tsar's brother, Constantine, the viceroy of Poland. The coup d'etat came to naught, but it sparked a plebeian insurrection. Thousands of armed civilians who had joined Wysocki's cadets in the streets of Warsaw kept on fighting until the insurrection hit every corner of the captive nation. There were many Poles who supported Constantine, particularly among the nobility, but Vincent Jastremski did not hesitate to join the revolutionaries. The fighting went on until September, 1831, when the czar's superior forces subdued the Polish uprising.

Obsessed by fear of assassination, Czar Nicholas sent spies, secret police and other authorities to arrest the leaders of the abortive revolution, closed the universities of Warsaw, Lublin and other cities, and took other measures to suppress the liberty-seeking Poles. To set an example the Iron Czar sent Wysocki in chains to Siberia with a sentence to serve twenty years at hard labor. Vincent Jastremski knew that the czar's agents were after him. During the brief period of carefree living that he enjoyed prior to 1831, he married a native girl and gave her a son.

Now, with Russian patrols returning to his native village daily to search for him, he felt that freedom was more important than his wife and child. He foiled the czar's noose by escaping to France.

For six or seven years, his movements were unknown to his young bride and his family. The French people, however, were happy to welcome Vincent Jastremski and other expatriates from Poland. They were grateful to the Polish volunteers who had come to France in Kosciuszko's time to help them fight for French independence. The young revolutionist from Kamienietz Podolski surfaced in the ancient town of Montpellier, eighty miles west of Marseilles, where on a clear day he could see the blue waters of the Mediterranean, the hardwood forests of the Pyrenees and the snow-capped Alps. He attended the famous medical school of the University of Montpellier, and on June 13, 1836, two months after he received his medical diploma, Louis Philippe, the king of France, honored him with a medal for his services in a cholera epidemic.[9]

Despite the importance of being a medical doctor he was forlorn, sad, and broken. He felt alone with his despair, like a lonely figure by the shore of a somber and hopeless ocean, until he met a young French girl, Ernestine Marguerite de Pointes, fourteen years younger than he was, and was driven by despair to marry her in 1838. No sooner had he tied the knot with her than his conscience bothered him. Did he now have two wives? His mother heard from him again. He had not heard from his first wife, Therese, for seven years, and he presumed, as judges do, when persons drop out of sight for such a long time, that she was dead. His hunch was right.

On October 18, 1838, his mother sat down with one of her sons, Justinian, and wrote a letter in Polish from Schtcherbowietz. The original letter is not now available. Mrs. Helm has a French translation of it in the Jastremski family papers and I had it translated into English. In the letter, which was originally in Justinian's handwriting, she notified her son, Vincent, "your former Therese ended her sad existence with tuberculosis in her doctor's nursing home." She did not say when Therese died. By implication, especially if her son was afflicted by the same disease, it was not long ago. Vincent's mother, whose first name was not given in the French version of the letter, said that Therese left "a poor boy as weak as a souffle and hopeless of living long. I keep him with me."

The information, though sad, eased Dr. Jastremski's mind. His mother reassured him. "The sacred bonds with your worthy wife are valid and legitimate," she said. "I am joyful because of this and I send my blessing to both of you, and we wish you a happy life full of good things."

Part of the original letter was in her own handwriting. At least a note in parentheses said so. But the letter I saw did not have what she wrote. The two short sentences which followed the remark were signed underneath by Blazej (Blaise), son of Louis Jastrzembski, and indicate sentiments of a man, not a woman. They read, "I embrace you, dear children. Your father who loves you till death."

Obviously, it looks as if Vincent was a son of Blazej and a grandson of Louis Jastrzembski. The postscript under Blazej's signature is even more remarkable. It indicates that Louis Jastrzembski died three years earlier three months shy of his 100th birthday. Thus it traces the male line of the family back to 1735. Altogether, projecting the genealogy of Leon Jastremski to 1974, there are eight generations, or heads of them, known to us.

No other letters or notes are extant of the family in Poland. The one Dr. Jastremski received in 1838 was treasured like a gilt-edged bond in a bank vault. From it he learned that as a result of a fall his mother was too weak to write all the letter herself. On account of her declining health she had a premonition that he would not hear from her again. She was closing her seventieth year of life.

"I cannot take pride in knowing any happiness in my life," Justinian wrote for her. "I have no rest from grief, either in my family or in my enemies. At my age, I am at the end of my power to defend myself against evil-doers. Your last letter made me quite sad as it told me that you also find evil persecutors in your way in your new position.

"You ask me, dear child, for news about myself and all the family. You will, therefore, learn with sorrow of the death of many relatives. My dear brother Casimir, judge of Uschitzk and later district tax collector at Jampol, died three years ago. His wife passed away before him. His daughter, Emilie, just married, died without issue, beautiful and adorned, in the springtime of her life, not having reached her 20th birthday. Kolski died three years ago. His wife, Anna, who is my sister, married again to P. Zabrda. She has a daughter by Kolski. As for me, thank God, I still live. My dear sons and your brothers, my dear Vincent, do not abandon me in my old age and they take my place in legal battles before the courts. May God and His Mother be praised! I am still well."

Justinian closed the letter with his own message. "Dear brother," he wrote, "be completely reassured, your new marriage is valid and legitimate. Live happily, you and your worthy wife. May you succeed as you desire. I am only adding a few words to this letter. Joseph has left for Kamienietz on business. Be well, my dear brother and sister-in-law. Love one another."

The union of the Polish exile and the descendant of an old aristocratic French family produced two sons. The first child, Jean Vincent, was born on August 15, 1839, in the village of Carbonne, department of Haute-Garonne, and the second one, Leon J., was born July 17, 1843, in Soulon, department of Ariege.[10]

Shortly after Leon's birth, Dr. Jastremski left the shores of Europe behind him forever. But not its memories. He had now been in France more than a decade and had come to love its culture and its language. He had contributed to the public health of the nation, had been successful by all common standards, and his fame had spread far and wide. Alexander Mouton, governor of Louisiana, with whom the king of France had been in communication, begged Louis Philippe to send him doctors, teachers, and immigrants. There had been a considerable flurry among his patients and friends when they heard he was about to forsake France for a former French possession in America. To the young doctor, these leave-takings were, for the most part, encouraging and happy.

But there was a question of taking Leon right away. He was too young for a rough voyage across the ocean, and an aunt offered to take care of him until he was old enough to travel. She lived in Carbonne, a village of about 1500 souls on the Garonne River about 23 miles southwest of Toulouse and about 27 miles north of Soulan, where Leon was born. His aunt and cousins probably took him to play in the garden of Calandre with two companions, Chourre and Auguste. In later years Vincent Castres, one of his cousins, relived those moments with him.[11]

Leon was to find his childhood years singularly devoid of fatherly advice and counsel. Dr. Jastremski and Ernestine and their first child, Jean (John), arrived in Vermilionville, Louisiana, as part of the steady trickle of immigrants from France.[12] The Moutons were waiting for him. On April 11, 1845, he bought a house from them at the corner of Vermilion and Saint John streets, with a view of the Catholic church, in the center of town.[13] The doctor was constantly away from his family, frantically seeking financial success and in the process leaving a tortuous trail of real estate transactions and punctuated with slave sales. During these years he had little time for his children. He loved them, but he was too occupied in securing their future to bother with their immediate needs for his sympathy and attention. His oldest son understood his preoccupation, but Leon, when he was brought from France at the age of six or seven, and sent to public school, was different. His doting aunt gave him more attention than was good for him, and when he came to Louisiana, he was a little show-off. He craved affection, and he desperately longed for an audience as in France. Denied his father's superfluous attention, he turned to his older brother, John, and the two had almost a father-and-son relationship for the rest of their lives.

Dr. Jastremski's life in Louisiana is better known than his life in France and Poland. His Polish experiences were of no use to him in Vermilionville, as the present town of Lafayette was known until 1884, and he was busier than ever in affairs alien to his early upbringing. Vermilionville, in the 1840's, seemed as pleasant a place of residence as any in the sugar bowl of Louisiana. One of its favorite sons, Alexander Mouton, ninth governor of Louisiana, and its people, many of whom were descendants of Acadian exiles, were proud of their existence under the flags of France, Spain, and the United States. Here, in southern Louisiana, Dr. Jastremski's life changed drastically.

He prospered in his medical practice and expanded his activities into other fields. He sold a drug store in 1848.[14] In 1850 he sold a 12-year-old mulatto boy by the name of William for $450,[15] and the following year he bought a 60-year-old slave, named Dick, for $100 at the home of the late Dame Celeste Braux.[16] Three years later he sold him for $300 to three merchants of Abbeville.[17] For a boy who never saw a Negro slave before the selling of slaves as if they were inhuman left quite an impression upon him. There was more meat for thought in them than in the patents of nobility—the descent from old Polish and French families—which came down to him from his parents. Practically every large landowner had slaves who served as house servants, coachmen and field hands.

The discovery of the slaves in the hands of Dr. Jastremski led me back to Mrs. Marion Moore Coleman's translation of Kalikst Wolski's memoirs, *American Impressions*,[18] for an examination of two Polish settlers whom he met at the home of Dr. Kajetan Kowalewski in New Orleans in 1852. Both Wolski and Kowalewski had taken part in the first post-partition uprising against Russia and, like Dr. Jastremski, ran away to escape the fate of Wysocki. Wolski fled to France, Kowalewski to Ireland, where he won the hand and heart of Mariah Dillon. With scarcely any warning in 1840 Kowalewski departed for New Orleans,[19] and as soon as his young bride and child reached him the next year, he moved to Pensacola, Florida, deserted them in Mobile, Alabama, and returned to New Orleans in 1846 to spend the last eighteen years of his life.[20]

Wolski did not give the names of the Poles he met in Dr. Kowalewski's home. "One of these lived around 100 kilometers from New Orleans, the other about 150," he wrote in his recollections which were published in an illustrated weekly *Klosy* (Ears of Grain) at Lwow, Poland, and, as Mrs. Coleman said, "subscribers in far-away Ukraine were as eager to get their copy every week as the citizens of the large cities. Some installments of "Podroz do Stanach Zjednoczonych" (Journey to the United States) could have reached the section in the Upper Dniester from which Dr. Jastremski came.

As Wolski continued, "One of the two spent all his time playing cards, the stakes being Negroes, so that he would win a Negro man or woman, or Negro children. These he would proceed to sell at once, so becoming on a small scale a dealer in Negroes."

I asked members of the Jastremski family if they ever heard this story in connection with Dr. Jastremski. None of them did. It probably does not refer to him. Mrs. Helm said that Dr. Vincent, as her great grandfather was called with a French mode of pronunciation, was too busy in his profession to engage in card games or slave buying. Of the three slaves that I found he owned, only the purchase of one was in the records of Lafayette Parish. The other two slaves were probably bought in another parish. Whatever discoveries are made in the future, the story of a Polish slave trader and a Polish abolitionist indicates that the conflict of ideologies permeated the lives of Polish settlers as well as other Americans. At least two Poles in Louisiana, Ignatius Szymanski in New Orleans and Theodore Rybicki in Donaldsonville, were known slave traders. Leon Jastremski was not isolated from this ideological warfare and probably shaped his own ideas from what he saw and heard in his new environment.

The settler Wolski described in his memoirs was, as I discovered, a parish surveyor and mapmaker, Joseph N. Gorlinski,[21] who married the daughter of Stanislaus Wrotnowski in Baton Rouge the first day of 1851. "Having come to America in 1845 or so," Wolski wrote, "he quickly obtained a well-paid position in some city office. He had been an artillery officer and was very capable. It was his job to make plans and engrave new maps of the recently acquired southwestern states. With the money he was able to save, each year he would buy two Negro children and set them free, doing this over a period of years and always complying with every formality of the law. In this way, by the time I was in New Orleans, he had managed to free more than twenty children, some boys, some girls. All these were now grown up and completely free, working for a living, surrounding their benefactor with blessings. None of them would leave the city in which he lived, as they all vied with each other in showing him their gratitude. This last Pole I have mentioned—the rest I had no feeling for and cut myself off from at once—invited me to visit him in his home.[22] And so once, when he was going there himself, I took him there by steamer."

In Baton Rouge, in the early 1850's, were a number of other Polish settlers. Except for Gorlinski, Wolski did not mention them. Valentina, the wife of Gorlinski, was born in southern France of Polish parents as were her brothers, Arthur and Stanislaus Wrotnowski, who eventually became Union officers during the Civil War. Their father, Stanislaus A. Wrotnowski, won eminence as Secretary of State at the same time. Among others who went to Baton Rouge[23] were B. Becinski,[24] a printer, A. Kowalski, a clerk, Francis Steckiewicz, a prison guard, Joseph Corwin,[25] a bookkeeper, Francis Lawryntowicz,[26] a medical doctor, Hypolite Oladowski, a gun expert at the U. S. Arsenal, and Rev. Joseph

Prachenski, a young Jesuit priest who served as an assistant at St. Joseph's Catholic Church from June 6, 1854, to August 24, 1857.

There were many varieties of Polish immigrants in Louisiana. Not all conformed to the mold patterned on the career of Szymanski or Gorlinski. They belonged to the forgotten thousands whose lives blended harmoniously into the Louisiana populace as they contributed their talents, great or small, to the growth and development of the state. In New Orleans, the Polish newcomers included August Pilitowski,[27] a watchmaker, Ignatius Skorupski, an artist in fireworks, Edward Bieganski, a prison guard,[28] M. Corwalski, a grocer, Gustavus Goslinski, a tailor, N. J. W. Kurczyn, a clerk, C. Lipinski, a confectioner, and Oscar Czarnowski, a pharmacist. The Polish settlers were an interesting and curious collection of individuals from all walks of life.[29] Such a catalogue of names as I have listed reveal, too, the tragedy of uprooted lives.

In April, 1854, when Leon Jastremski was nine, his father sold the house the family occupied nine years in Vermilionville to Michel Crouchet, a French immigrant, for $1800 and moved to Abbeville, the capital of the adjoining parish of Vermilion.[30] Eternally restless, Dr. Jastremski could always think of a reason for moving to a different town, or even a different continent, and find it superior to the one he left. He probably moved to Abbeville because it had no medical doctor and he wanted to be the first one. There were a few medical doctors in Vermilionville, and leaving it the citizens would not be deprived of such attention as he gave them. The highlights of his years in Lafayette parish were pieced together from court records in Lafayette, but it turned to a blur in Vermilion parish.

If Dr. Jastremski left a will, records of slave sales, signed a deed or a mortgage, all the legal documents from the beginning of Abbeville in a new parish in 1850 were destroyed when the court house burned down early in 1885.

Abbeville, founded by a Capuchin missionary, Abbe A. D. Megret, reminded Leon Jastremski of a French provence town. The square in front of the Catholic church, which was named for St. Marie Madeleine, was flanked by little stores, shops, and offices. Narrow streets ran in all directions from the court house. Dr. Jastremski bought one of the lots between the bayou Vermilion and Main Street, then known as Rue des Beaux Arts, and built a house to accommodate his family and his medical practice. For a while John and Leon Jastremski enjoyed the quiet village. They played on the bayou behind their home or raced their vehicles down the street parallel with the cemetery behind the Catholic chapel.

Then quite suddenly the immigrant parents of the two teenagers were dead. No record of Ernestine Jastremski's death was listed in the Death Register of St. Marie Madeleine as was Dr. Jastremski. Leon, in political biographies of his life, said she died just before his father.[31] Dr. Jastremski died September 29, 1856,[32] and was buried in the cemetery across the street from his last home. No grave markers, or even location of the grave, exist. The last sign I found of Mrs. Jastremski was May 22, 1856, when she visited the home of Madame V. Boissier in Vermilionville for money due from Vincent and Octave Bertrand, who acted as their agents in the sale of property in Vermilionville.[33]

The dissolution of the Jastremski fortune is as misty as a gossamer floating in air. Neither John nor Leon ever said what happened to the home on Rue des Beaux Arts and other possessions in Abbeville. When John moved to Baton Rouge in 1858, he was apparently ready to forget that he ever lived in Abbeville. On June 27, 1859, in the village of Plaquemine, across the Mississippi River from Baton Rouge, he married Leontine Keays, daughter of Jean and Henrietta (nee Henry) Keays, with Rev. Francis C. Follot, pastor of St. John the Evangelist Catholic Church, performing the ceremony,[34] and lived in Baton Rouge the rest of his life. Leon's life was more variable.

Had the first court house of Vermilion parish not burned down, one would have a listening post to one of the most interesting intrigues in Abbeville. The appointment of Jean Pierre Gueydan, a 27-year-old French storekeeper in Abbeville, as a tutor to the two heirs of Dr. Jastremski was among the papers that went up in flames with the court house. After coming to New Orleans in 1850, Gueydan opened a mercantile house with another French immigrant and sold goods by driving from village to village in southern Louisiana until he settled with his wife and two small children in Abbeville.[35] He was at the same time interested in cattle and cotton. During the Civil War he served as captain of the Home Guards in Abbeville. In 1895 he laid out the town of Gueydan in Vermilion parish and died a wealthy man in Paris in 1900.

As tutor to Dr. Jastremski's heirs Gueydan was taken to court by Francois Gastal, who lived next door to the Jastremski property, and the court's decision was against the estate.[36] The number of the docket which was burned was 662. On May 7, 1860, Alexander Lege, sheriff of Vermilion parish, sold the Jastremski property for $345 to Valerie, wife of Eugene I. Guegnon,[37] editor and publisher of the *Abbeville Meridional,* where Leon had started out as a printer's devil in 1856. At the time of the sheriff's sale to satisfy Gastal's suit, Leon and the *Meridional* were split.[38] It is not known if the lawsuit had anything to do with it.

So far as Jean Gueydan was concerned Leon never mentioned him, although each devoted the next four decades of their lives to the promotion of Louisiana. Gueydan's handling of the Jastremski estate remains a mystery.

Whatever Dr. Jastremski left to his children, probably nothing mattered as much to us as John and Leon Jastremski. These were the children by which Vincent and Marguerite Ernestine gave the Jastremski name to all America.[39]

3

The Big Soldier

THE story of the people who took part in the Civil War will probably never be ended.

The role that Leon Jastremski played in it earned him a plethora of encomiums. He was called "Louisiana's greatest Pole,"[1] "a patriotic and useful citizen,"[2] "a notable Pole in the South,"[3] "a gallant Confederate,"[4] and "a man of strong character and dauntless courage."[5] James Ryder Randall, author of "Maryland, My Maryland," a rallying song of the Confederacy, wrote that he "keeps the lamp of chivalry alight in hearts of gold."[6] At one time or another the gallant follower of Generals Robert E. Lee and "Stonewall" Jackson no doubt deserved each one of these tributes. He was also described as faithful, reliable, exact, obedient, devout, loyal, generous and courageous. To his descendants he was known simply as "the big soldier."[7]

He was seventeen when the war clouds rolled over the bayous of Louisiana. In the center of things sat one of the richest planters of the state, Alexander Mouton, whom he had known since his arrival from France, and everyone looked upon him to reach a decision involving their future. He presided at a convention in 1861 when Louisiana seceded from the Union and joined the Confederate States. Almost immediately, in various parishes, military companies were formed for immediate service under the Pelican flag.

Leon Jastremski had a desire to go in a hurry, but he was unable to raise a company of volunteers in Vermilion parish to go with him.[8] Had he stayed in Vermilionville, the present town of Lafayette, he would have been perhaps in the Confederate army before the bombardment of Fort Sumter. Raising a company there, owing to the pace the Moutons set in volunteering for service, was easier than in Abbeville.

The inhabitants of Abbeville influenced to a large extent his behavior. The fear of economic ruin and loss of political prestige made many of them wary of a sectional war. Understanding them was not such a hard job for the young immigrant, but he realized that in the event of war he would be better off if he knew how to drill and handle arms. He joined with seventy men and boys in Abbeville to form a quasi-military organization and to learn the rudiments of military life. The sound of the drum and the voice of command in the streets of this little town on the Vermilion River each morning and evening filled him with ardor and patriotism. Their drillmaster was a Frenchman who had learned the rudiments of military training in the French army.[9]

The bombardment of Fort Sumter, which began on April 12, 1861, was not enough to send Leon Jastremski to a Confederate recruiter. "As soon as the war begins," he wrote to his brother on May 20, "I will quit my work and go to enlist in some good company."[10]

The job he had in Abbeville is, owing to the discovery of the letter of May 20, 1861, subject to a new interpretation. In July, when he went with a companion to Camp Moore to enlist in the Confederate army, he listed his occupation as a printer, but in his letter to his brother he said that when he enlisted he would "abandon the mortar to take up the rifle and sabre." By referring to a mortar, he gave us an impression that he was a drugstore clerk and crushed or pounded substances in a druggist's bowl-like vessel with a pestle.[11]

His job prospects were not particularly bright in the years behind him. On the death of his parents in 1856, he entered the printing shop of the *Meridional,* a weekly newspaper owned by Eugene I. Guignon, a stormy Frenchman, and served an apprenticeship at the case. He apparently left the newspaper plant to accept a job in Baton Rouge. His stay there was brief. He left Baton Rouge late in 1860 to look for work in New Orleans. He saw in a newspaper that a new newspaper in Liberty, Mississippi, called *L'Amite Democrat* needed a printer and he applied for the job. He worked there three weeks and returned to New Orleans because the newspaper owner did not have enough money to pay him. Again he looked for work in the printing shops and pharmacies of New Orleans, but without success. He heard that James Bradley had need of a clerk in Abbeville and applied for the job.[12] Not long after he returned to Abbeville he spoke of working with a mortar and again when he was facing a cold winter in Virginia he mentioned that Bradley sent him two blankets.[13] With such a background, it would be more accurate to say he was a drugstore clerk, not a printer, when he enlisted on July 22, 1861, as a private in Company E, the Louisiana Swamp Rifles, of the Tenth Regiment of Louisiana Volunteers.

Physically, Private Jastremski looked like a human string bean. He was five feet, eleven inches tall, but grew another inch by the time he reached maturity. From his mother he inherited his dark hair and black eyes. From his father he got a certain humanitarian and idealistic slant on life which, together with his family pride and his Southern sympathies, made his character, even in its formative period, a combination of weird contradictions.[14]

Although his father spelled the family name phonetically when he arrived in Louisiana, Leon Jastremski's name appeared in company records in such distorted forms as Jasdremski, Jastraupski, Jastramski, Jardremsky, Strawenski, Jastermiskie, and Gestremsky. It never was spelled Jastrzebski as it was in Poland.

Dominant in the young soldier's character was the inbred belief that being a Jastremski, or Jastrzebski, blessed with the rank of nobility and prestige, he was born to fight for his rights and liberties. This belief, however, was to be used for Confederate rights and liberties. Mixed up with this were all the characteristics which ordinarily accrue from a life in a Louisiana parish. He was surrounded by rich planters, slave owners and their influences. Yet despite this environment, and partly because of his Polish lineage, he was able to keep a liberal and detached view on life such as most children of European parents lost when they moved to a new country.

The Tenth Louisiana Infantry, under the command of Colonel Mandeville de Marigny, left for Virginia four days after Jastremski enlisted, in two sections of box cars, and, after arrival in Richmond on August 5, was attached to General John B. Magruder's army on the treacherous peninsula between the James and York rivers in the southeastern corner of the state.[15] Starting as a private, Jastremski rose step by step until Colonel Marigny promoted him on February 23, 1862, to the vacancy which had occurred in the position of regimental Sergeant Major.[16] Shortly afterwards, the rigors of handling the regiment prompted Colonel Marigny to resign, and Eugene Waggaman, a tough but conceited sugarcane planter from New Orleans, Louisiana, succeeded him. He was the son of George A. Waggaman, U. S. Senator from Louisiana when Andrew Jackson was president and twenty years after serving under him in the War of 1812 at New Orleans. Young Waggaman was still a child when his father, a great Whig leader, "fell in a duel" in 1843.

During the period he spent on the Virginia peninsula, first in a tent camp known as Camp Squatley, six miles out of Williamsburg, and then in Camp Marigny at Lee's Mills on the Warwick River, he had plenty of time to spend around the campfire and become acquainted with his comrades in arms. He admired a sabre that one of them had and exchanged a French-made Lefaucheux revolver for it. He liked to read newspapers from Louisiana. Sporadically he wrote letters to his brother in Baton Rouge, first in French and later in English, detailed his duties and promotions, activities of his regiment, preparations for war, and other news. "The peninsula is a very critical place," he wrote in French, "and it is necessary for us to fight heroically in order to achieve victory."[17]

To protect the Confederate capital, Magruder sent his army, numbering roughly 9,000 officers and enlisted men and divided into eight brigades to lay out a string of batteries and entrenchments in the peninsula lying east of Richmond and to resist any Union expedition that tried to occupy it. He called upon a young, colorful Polish surveyor from New Orleans, Colonel Valery Sulakowski, who looked like a hero out of Victor Hugo's "Ninety-Three," to command the Seventh Brigade, consisting of the Tenth and Fourteenth Louisiana Infantry.[18] Magruder and Sulakowski apparently impressed Jastremski so much that he started to grow a mustache similar to theirs and never removed it. The hot-tempered brigade leader supervised the construction of a defense line that a Union engineer who tackled it shortly afterwards called "one of the most extensive known to modern times."[19] As Jastremski indicated in a letter to his brother, the brigade had about 100 Negroes to dig rifle trenches, breastworks, and other fortifications, and at times he supervised their work.[20] Sulakowski, however, left the brigade before his engineering works were ever tested.

The Seventh Brigade was not the first Confederate outfit to use able-bodied slaves in the construction of its military defenses. From the very beginning of hostilities every Confederate general from the Potomac to the Gulf knew he had the authority to impress slaves into service. On September 7, 1861, Magruder, one of the South's most popular generals, called upon slaveowners in southeastern Virginia to send him half of their slaves with picks, shovels, and axes. "The Negroes will be allowed 50¢ a day and plenty of provisions," he said, "the money to be paid by the quartermaster to their masters." The amount paid to slaveowners varied from 25¢ a day for a water boy to $2.00 a day for a slave, horse and cart. Common laborers averaged 50¢ a day.

The Tenth Louisiana Infantry didn't see much fighting until Major General George B. McClellan, the slow, fastidious head of the Union Army of the Potomac, met the regiment on the banks of the Warwick River in April of 1862. McClellan had a well-organized army of 100,000 men, but, instead of taking Richmond quickly, he had trouble with the strong batteries and sturdy Southerners in his road. For nearly three months the Confederates delayed his march to Richmond and used the time to recruit more men, cripple McClellan and save Richmond. During this period Jastremski took part in the engagements at Dam No. 1 on April 16, Williamsburg on May 4, and Savage Station on June 29.

The biggest battle of the campaign in which he took part was in the night charge of his regiment at Malvern Hill, the last of the Seven Days' Battles which took place on the north bank of the James River about 18 miles southeast of Richmond. Just before it occurred Robert E. Lee, a dignified, magnanimous and skillful Virginian, succeeded to the command of the Confederate army in Virginia, formally known as the Army of Northern Virginia. Lee had spent all of the first day of July in vainly assaulting McClellan's position on Malvern Hill and his losses were heavy. He held the Tenth Louisiana in reserve, and as only a little bit of the sun was left, everybody in the regiment felt that it would not be brought into action. Like them, Jastremski heard the men chaffing each other as they lay in a ravine out of the line of fire from Union gunboats in the James River. The mood of the regiment rapidly changed when someone brought a note to Colonel Waggaman.[21]

When the Colonel shouted, "Fall in!" the men came out of the ravine like a swarm of bees. The commander had a great reputation as a fighter and his men would follow him into any battle without flinching from danger. Sometimes he carried a cane instead of a sword into a battle, but it did not make any difference to Jastremski and the other members of the Tenth Louisiana.[22] They followed him over the crest of a hill by which they were protected from shells all day and straight across an open field. The fire of shells from the Union battery on Malvern Hill and from the gunboats in the James River grew heavier. But Colonel Waggaman did not stop. "By the left flank," he shouted, and the Tenth moved quickly along the edge of the field toward the spewing cannons on the plateau. The artillery fire escalated.[23]

Within 300 yards of the Union battery, Colonel Waggaman halted the regiment, placed it in another ravine, and awaited further orders and additional help. Eventually a courier on horseback brought an order.

Colonel Waggaman walked into the middle of his regiment, drew his sword, and said:

"Men, we are ordered to charge the cannon in our front and take them. The Tenth Regiment has been in reserve all week, and every other Louisiana regiment has been in action. All of them have distinguished themselves, and I trust that the Tenth will not be the first to falter. Not a shot must be fired until we get to the guns. Now, men, we are going to charge. Remember Butler and the women of New Orleans. Forward, charge!"[24]

Before anyone could say the commander's name the regiment was on a ridge opposite the cannon-crowned plateau. Men fell on every side as they entered a storm of grape and canister and musketry fire. Others kept going to the shouts of "Butler, Butler," until they reached the Federal line. At least 500 Louisianians made it and captured ten Union cannons.

No sooner had it happened than Colonel Waggaman saw another Federal line moving toward him. It was the 69th New York Infantry. "Fire," he ordered, and the muskets of the Tenth Lousiana forced the Irish regiment from New York to go back.

"Lie down, men," Colonel Waggaman then ordered, "we'll wait for our reinforcements."

If Lee, Magruder, or someone else had the responsibility and sent a fresh brigade to relieve the Tenth Louisiana, he could have stampeded the main part of McClellan's army. It should have happened. It could have happened. It didn't happen. The charge of the Tenth had already caused a panic in the Federal ranks. Some general had left the regiment alone to wrestle with the Northerners.

Colonel Waggaman did not realize he was a victim of no Confederate co-ordination until a withering volley raked his regiment from right to left. Sitting next to Jastremski, he thought the fire came from another Confederate regiment. "For God's sake, Sergeant Major," he said to Jastremski, "go to those men and tell them to cease firing; they are killing their own men."

As the result of obeying the order, Jastremski fell into the hands of the enemy. By the glare of the second volley, Waggaman discovered that his regiment was being enfiladed not by Confederate troops but by the Twelfth U. S. Regulars and the 69th New York Infantry. There was a brief struggle at close quarters. The survivors of this charge fell back down the bloody slope. In addition to Jastremski, thirty enlisted men, Colonel Waggaman and a lieutenant were captured by the two Union regiments. Many officers and men were killed. Scores of others were wounded. The charge of the Tenth Louisiana on the deadly incline ranked with the charge of the British Light Brigade at Balaklava in Crimea.

Jastremski spent a short time as a prisoner of war in Fort Delaware, and when he was exchanged August 5, 1862, he hurried back to the Tenth Louisiana Infantry, now with other Louisiana regiments under Stonewall Jackson's command. The fourth day after his exchange he found himself in the battle of Cedar Mountain near Culpeper, Virginia. He trod a wheat field where blood had just been spilled, and took cover in a grove, when the Tenth was ordered to form a line of battle. As he came out of the woods, Jastremski was captured again.

His career in the Confederate Army was so far a nightmare. He saw no battles in the first nine months of service, and now, in less than two months, he was in five battles, but captured in two of them. How long would misfortune follow him?

He was exchanged shortly after the Army of Northern Virginia beat Pope's army at Cedar Mountain and returned to his company in time to take part in the second battle of Manassas (Bull Run) on August 28-30, in time to proceed with his command in Stonewall Jackson's march to the rear of General Pope's army. He felt a little better after this battle because the Southerners were again victorious. Pope's army retreated to Washington.

General Lee then prepared to invade Maryland. No sooner had Jastremski and his comrades left Manassas to follow Lee than Jackson stopped them at a crossroads in Fairfax County, Virginia, and said, "Louisianians, I need you once more."[25] The gray-clad soldiers filled their muskets with powder that they had taken from the pouches of those who were killed at Manassas and engaged in a brief, but wild and bloody, fight in the rain at Ox Hill, or, as it is more popularly known, Chantilly, on September 1.

Four days later, when they crossed the Potomac at White's Ford, they sang "Maryland, My Maryland." By moving the Army of Northern Virginia into Maryland, Lee hoped to swing the people of that border state to the side of the Confederacy, to strengthen anti-war activities in the North, to draw Union troops from other areas, and to relieve Virginia for a time of the ravages of war. But the minds of his young soldiers were not on such things.

Frederick, a small city of some importance in the wheat belt of the Maryland Piedmont, was the first civilized town Lee's soldiers had seen for many months. The girls they saw on the streets of Frederick were attractive. The stores were well stocked. After the Confederate troops had passed through the city, the public officials complained to Stonewall Jackson that his troops behaved worse than animals. They charged that their stores were plundered and their women raped.[26]

Jackson replied that if their charges were true he would punish the culprits. He ordered the Louisiana troops to return to Frederick for the purposes of identification, but the commander of the Louisianians refused to obey the order unless it included all the troops that had been in Frederick. He was arrested. Nothing else was done.

The invasion of Maryland required the Confederates to move their supply lines across the Blue Ridge Mountains and center them in the Shenandoah Valley. Lee figured that if his army could seize Harper's Ferry, a town in what is now West Virginia and made famous by John Brown's raid of the U. S. arsenal in 1859, he could secure his line of communications for further advance to the North.

Early on September 15 the Confederate forces hurled shells on Union positions from all sides and within a matter of hours captured the U. S. arsenal. Jastremski and his companions had fun after this engagement when they took off their ragged, torn gray-colored uniforms and clothed their bodies in the Union blues they had found in the arsenal.[27]

Many of them had blue uniforms on when they were called to join their comrades at Sharpsburg (Antietam). With his back to the Potomac River, Lee had 19,000 men immediately available to form his battle lines, but he faced an enemy army almost twice his numbers. His lines were hit by galling fire and driven back, foot by foot, yard by yard, when they were reinforced by more Southerners and drove against the Federal troops until they gained some of the ground they had lost. Lee shifted and added to his forces until he had about 41,000 Confederates under his command. His opponent, McClellan, had 87,000.

The battle of September 17, 1862, was the bloodiest single day of the war. Jastremski was with the 2nd Louisiana Brigade that, in a crushing counterattack, saved Lee's right flank from collapse, but out of the 2700 Confederates killed in that battle, four officers and 71 enlisted men were from his brigade.

Sharpsburg was a severe blow to the Confederate cause. It changed the entire aspect of the war from a political affair to preserve the union to a crusade to free the slaves. It ended Lee's hope that Maryland would join the Confederacy. Popular sentiment in Europe swung to the side of the North and destroyed the South's last hope of foreign assistance.

"Most important of all," said Henry and Dana Lee Thomas, "it gave Lincoln the psychological moment for the Emancipation Proclamation."[28]

It also changed Jastremski's status. General Jackson ordered the filling of the vacancies among the line officers, and on September 20, the Louisiana regiment, sadly thinned in ranks, transferred him to Company H, otherwise known as the Orleans Blues, and elevated him to the rank of 1st Lieutenant.[29]

Now a path was available to the Federal troops which, if they could exploit it, would lead to the very vitals of the Confederacy. The fate of the Confederacy depended upon roadblocks, skirmishes, and other actions of Lee's army, and Jastremski spent most of his time in the final quarter of 1862 in such delaying tactics. Such towns as Martinsburg,

Ripley, Winchester, Berryville, Strasburg, Edinburg, Thornton Gap, and Madison were visited in his marches.[30]

Fredericksburg, situated halfway between Washington and Richmond in Virginia, was a major objective of both armies, and Jastremski fought there on December 13 when Lee successfully defended his position with 78,000 almost famished, suffering soldiers.[31] It was not always so. Fredericksburg changed hands seven times in four years and was one of the bloodiest battlegrounds of history.

Early in May, 1863, Lee again risked his army of 62,000 men in a headlong clash at Chancellorsville, about ten miles west of Fredericksburg. The Army of the Potomac under the command of General Joseph Hooker had 130,000 troops. When Lincoln saw Hooker a short time before, he said, "In your next battle put in all your men."[32] Lee pinned the execution of his strategy on Jackson, the ablest and greatest flanker that the war ever saw, and the fighting qualities of his soldiers. He outflanked an army superior in numbers and equipment and rolled them up like a scroll. Jastremski helped Jackson to crush the right of the Union Army, but the two were wounded, Jastremski in the throat on May 3. "By 10 a. m.," Lee wrote in his report on May 4, "we were in full possession of the field."[33]

When he got well, Jastremski returned to his company and became its captain. Now his soldiers were under the command of General Eugene S. Ewell. The next battle in which he saw action was on June 15 when Ewell had to get Federal troops out of Winchester, near the northern entrance to the Shenandoah Valley, because crops and cattle and factories made the valley an important requisitioning area for the Confederacy.

Shortly afterwards Lee's bugle once more sounded for invasion of the North. Jastremski found the invasion of Maryland less dangerous than the first time, and the troops under Ewell invaded Pennsylvania virtually unopposed. The populous towns of Chambersburg, Carlisle, and Shippensburg, boasting of their quotas in Lincoln's volunteer arm, were suddenly lifted by Southern soldiers from obscurity to take their places in history. Near one of these Pennsylvania towns Jastremski read a message to his company from Lee: "No troops could have displayed greater fortitude or better performed the arduous marches of the past ten days." Lee wrote the words at Chambersburg.[34]

The new commander of the Army of the Potomac, General George G. Meade, hastened up from Maryland to locate and fight Lee's army. Jastremski was in an uneasy position. In the past ten months he had fought in four great battles—Bull Run, Sharpsburg, Fredericksburg and Chancellorsville. The last two had raised "in an extraordinary manner the spirit of the army."[35] Jackson had been Jastremski's commander in all four, and now with a fifth battle approaching he had a one-legged commander with a bald head. Was he a "re-animate Jackson," as the newspapers called him?

The battle of Gettysburg would test their ability. Jastremski's company was almost famished, the wagons not being able to keep up, and were ill-clothed as were the rest of Ewell's soldiers.

On the eve of one of the Civil War's most decisive conflicts, an agent of the Sanitary Commission saw one of Ewell's camps and his description could fit Captain Jastremski's company as well as any other company in the same brigade.[36] "Their dress was a wretched mixture of all cuts and colors. Every man seemed to have on whatever he could get hold of, without regard to shape or color. . . . Their shoes were poor; some of the men were entirely barefooted. Their equipments were light. They consisted of a thin woolen blanket, coiled up and slung from the shoulder in the form of a sash, a haversack swung from the opposite shoulder, and a cartridge box. The whole cannot weigh more than twelve or fourteen pounds."

The agent asked one of Ewell's soldiers if he had no shelter tent, and the soldier replied, "I just wouldn't tote one."

Like Washington's soldiers at Valley Forge in 1777, a few of Jastremski's soldiers probably marched barefooted to Gettysburg. His company marched about thirty miles,[37] and when it arrived early in the afternoon Ewell took it and other companies right away into heavy fighting without any rest. They took a position on the Confederate left. By nightfall Ewell's troops occupied the small market town lying between two low ridges eight miles north of the Mason-Dixon line. The soldiers in blue retreated southward to Cemetery Hill.

Ewell was afterwards criticized for not advancing and taking Culp's

Hill at the southeast end of Gettysburg that evening.[38] Historians claimed that his soldiers "could easily have crossed it and would have been at the Union rear. Perhaps a direct frontal assault could have swept the shattered Union army from the summit of Cemetery Ridge and a retreat turned into a rout."[39] Jastremski, however, knew no man could fight all the time. His troops, having marched 30 miles under sweltering heat, and fought two stubborn Union corps in one day, were worn out like beasts in a Biblical drought.

The following day Ewell's troops tried to take Culp's Hill, but Meade's troops resisted their advance. Jastremski was wounded there in the arm. His company renewed the fighting for Culp's Hill the third day, but when the town trembled in the afternoon under the heaviest artillery duel ever fought in this country, Lee decided to withdraw his army from Gettysburg. Of the 159,000 who fought at Gettysburg, more than 50,000 were casualties.

Meade failed to annihilate Lee's remaining troops in their retreat from Gettysburg. The Confederates used the time that followed the major conflict to nurse their wounds and rebuild their forces. Jastremski spent three weeks in September at General Hospital No. 4, Richmond, and was treated for the wounds in his throat and right hand.[40] He fought one more battle in 1863 when, on November 27, Meade tried to maneuver the Confederates out of position along the Rapidan River, but, finding no assailable point in the Confederate line, he withdrew his forces.

The two armies camped not far away, with the Rapidan River between them, in the winter of 1863-64. The soldiers relaxed, smoked, played games, took furloughs and generally had a good time until the spring of 1864 when General Ulysses S. Grant, a slouchy, round-shouldered, complex officer in a black sugar-loaf hat, arrived in Culpeper, Virginia, and planned to fight Lee's Army of Northern Virginia wherever possible. James Longstreet, one of Lee's officers, said, "That man will fight us every day and every hour till the end of the war."[41]

Captain Jastremski found his duties growing heavier and heavier. Defending the southern bank of the Rapidan, picketing the main road between Fredericksburg and Orange Court House, engaging in skirmishes with the enemy in various places, meeting with officers of the Tenth Louisiana regiment, issuing orders and making brief speeches to his soldiers took up most of his time. There were fewer campfires, less lounging in shirt sleeves, smoking of pipes, and washing of clothes. By keeping on the go, they missed on one occasion from being surrounded by Federal troops and captured. The captain from Abbeville held his company together as well as he could.

The appearance of Grant raised speculation that he would move the Army of the Potomac out of camp, across the Rapidan, and into the Wilderness, a dense chapparal that stretched for six miles from the river of ghosts to Spotsylvania, "to try again what four previous attempts had failed to do—crush Lee's army and capture Richmond."[42]

On April 30, the day that Jastremski's company left its winter quarters near Pisgah Church, President Lincoln wrote to General Grant, "I am very anxious that any great disaster, or the capture of our men in great numbers, shall be avoided."[43] The letter probably made Grant nervous. The battles he fought often cost an appalling number of lives. Someone said that when the battle of the Wilderness began on May 5, Grant smoked cigars and whittled sticks all day long.[44]

In six days of hard fighting Grant pushed Lee, by a smashing, head-on attack, from one end of the wild, tangled woodland between the Rapidan River and Spotsylvania to the other, and poured men into the campaign as if he had unlimited manpower. Despite heavy casualties, he wrote, "I propose to fight it out on this line if it takes all summer."[45]

Woodward called this battle "the bloodiest military enterprise in American history." Ewell, who bore the brunt of the conflict at the "bloody angle," near Spotsylvania, was unable to hold off the tremendous attack of three divisions led by General W. S. Hancock. On May 12, Captain Jastremski was captured along with most of General Edward Johnston's Division. Union General John Sedgwick was one of about 29,000 casualties.

As Captain Jastremski was taken again to Fort Delaware, dark forebodings passed one after the other like clouds across his mind. At three different times he was captured, but returned to the Tenth Louisiana again and again, and now, at the age of twenty years, he wondered if he would return to the scene of conflict the fourth time. Gloom filled the Confederate ranks. Grant weakened Lee and his army, and permitted the Confederates no rest. Without knowing how many months he would spend as a prisoner of war, Captain Jastremski himself was the first to recognize its significance, and he hated to think of the chances that it would close his military career.

To draw the curtain on his military career is to obscure the final surrender of the Confederate forces and the return of the war-worn veterans to their distant and desolate homes. The number of men who surrendered in the Tenth Louisiana is not known. Nearly one-fourth of the 845 men who enrolled in it were murdered, killed in battle, and died of disease.[46] Many, like Jastremski, were in Northern prisons, and so did not feel the joy of their ragged, dirty and penniless comrades on their return to Louisiana. They sang:

> Here's a smile for those who love me,
> A tear for those who hate;
> And whatever sky's above me,
> Here's a heart for every fate.

4

Prisoner of War

LITTLE is known of the experiences Leon Jastremski shared with other Confederate prisoners when he first landed on Pea Patch Island. As a Sergeant Major in the Tenth Louisiana Infantry, he was probably treated the same as any other enlisted man from the South who was confined in a Northern prison. He didn't rate special attention.

Shortly after his capture at Malvern Hill, he was herded together with other Confederate prisoners and shipped northward on a heavily-guarded steamer. Coming up the Delaware, he strained his eyes to catch the first glimpse of Fort Delaware. When the low silhouette of the fort hove above the green waters in a bend of the river, a single panoramic sweep of his eyes beheld the sandy beaches of New Jersey to his right, an inlet to Delaware City to the west, and a small, low and marsh-fringed island directly ahead. Almost Louisianian in character, the island, originally a small mud shoal, gradually accumulated more mud, sprigs, and, as its name indicates, peas, until it covered over sixty acres only a few feet above the water line.

As it stands now, Fort Delaware, begun in 1833 and completed in 1859, spread out like a gray-colored, five-sided layer cake with a big hole in the center on six acres of Pea Patch Island in the middle of the Delaware River. The walls of the fort were built of granite and brick, and their low-cut lines and form help them to fit amiably into the scene of green meadows and trees and cattails that divide the fort from the waters of the Delaware. With a facade of clear gray granite, the walls rise thirty-two feet from a weed-choked moat that surrounds it.[1]

Major John Sanders, a short, stubby engineer who had served in the Mexican War with Gen. Zachary Taylor's army, designed Fort Delaware for three tiers of guns between five castle-like bastions.[2] A visitor who now leisurely explores the damp casemates, with arched brick walls, and the grass-covered ramparts can still see the ingenuity of his design. He found places in every important nook of the fort for casemates and barbettes along the parapet.

Inside the fort and parallel with two walls to the left of the sally port were two brick buildings, three stories high, in which the garrison was quartered. The building adjacent to the sally port was the enlisted men's barracks. The three rows of windows in the granite walls were long and narrow and were different in appearance from the wide gun embrasures on two levels between them and the bastions. The first floor contained the kitchen and mess facilities, with sleeping quarters on the two upper floors. The other building, almost perpendicular to the enlisted men's barracks but not joined to it, was smaller. The administrative offices of the garrison were located on the first floor. The officers of Fort Delaware and their families lived on the two upper floors. The parade ground originally covered nearly two acres of space in the center of the fort.

The garrison started out with twenty men in February, 1861, when Captain Augustus A. Gibson, a young West Point graduate with a vast knowledge of artillery, became the commanding officer of Fort Delaware. The number jumped to 230 by late summer when fifty regular army artillerymen and eighty volunteers organized as Independent Battery A were assigned to the garrison. Among the officers of the artillery company was a young Polish artist, Stanislaus Mlotkowski, then a lieutenant, but later, March 1, 1862, when he took charge of the battery, a captain.[3] With a furious energy that unquestionably shortened his life, Captain Mlotkowski threw himself into the routine by calling his company together on the parade ground and holding constant artillery practice.

By the time Mlotkowski arrived on September 19, 1861,[4] each casement in the lower tier of the fort had a heavy cannon, a 32-pound Columbiad, which could be moved on a track for crossfiring through iron bound embrasures overlooking the Delaware. Altogether there were twenty Columbiads in the casements, twenty howitzers on the barbettes, and assorted other guns throughout the castellated work. An intricate system of passages and stairways in the bastions tied the casemates and barbettes to the nerve center of the garrison.

As the Confederates did not try to capture Fort Delaware, the quietude of the fort, combined with the waters surrounding the island, acted like a sleeping pill on the garrison the first year of the war. The officers and men had little to do with the enemy until 258 Confederate prisoners of war were brought to the fort in April, 1862. The fort was not designed to handle prisoners of war. Despite Captain Gibson's objections, he was answerable for them. By shifting the personnel of the garrison to different quarters, he locked the prisoners behind thick, brass-studded doors of the fort until a wooden shed was built in the eastern end of the parade ground.

The carpenters who showed up on Pea Patch Island did not end their work with one building. They were assigned to put up more buildings for prisoners. When the first set was completed, Colonel William Hoffman, Commissary General of Prisoners, wrote to Secretary of War Stanton on June 15 that he inspected the buildings and found "accommodations there for 2,000 prisoners," but only 600 were there. "The island is a very suitable place for the confinement of prisoners of war," he continued, "and I recommend . . . sheds for 3,000 more prisoners."[5]

Captains Gibson and Mlotkowski were still there when Jastremski arrived on Pea Patch Island early in July. He arrived there with little more than the clothes on his back and a Pelican souvenir in his pocket. The saber he prized like an old family heirloom was gone. It was taken from him by his captors at Malvern Hill just as Colonel Waggaman lost his silver-hilted sword. He met prisoners at Fort Delaware from other parts of the South, but principally from Maryland and Virginia.

If he had the education of John Bunyan, the English religious writer, he might have written while confined in a Northern prison a great American testament. Bunyan wrote the imperishable *Pilgrim's Progress* when confined in an English jail.

At first glance, however, he was depressed with what he saw. The prisoners were treated no better than the Northern prisoners in the Confederate prison at Andersonville, Georgia. The barracks were dirty and surrounded by filth and vermin. The food was terrible. The prisoners suffered from malnutrition, contagious diseases, and unhealthy conditions. Eventually the death rate at Fort Delaware was higher than at any other Northern prison and it was called the Andersonville of the North.

Ordinarily the prisoners were fed twice a day. When they dug ditches, unloaded ships, carried boards, pushed wheelbarrows, pulled carts, or helped the workmen in the construction of the buildings on the island, they got an extra ration.

The island was a beehive of activity when Jastremski came. In July, the number of prisoners[6] on it jumped from 1,260 to 3,434. The rapid influx of prisoners gave Captain Gibson fits. He had less than 300 guards for more than 3,000 prisoners. On July 12, eight days after Jastremski's arrival, 19 prisoners escaped from the island. They were followed the next night by 200 more, but official reports listed none. As the result of the numerous escapes, Captain Gibson was transferred. He passed his troubles to Major Henry S. Burton, an experienced administrator.

Jastremski was among 3,059 prisoners who left Fort Delaware at the beginning of August. Within a week of his exchange, he returned to the Tenth Louisiana Infantry and was surprised to find that Colonel Waggaman had fared better as a prisoner of war than he did. Waggaman told him how he got his sword back on his release from Fort Warren.

The Colonel described how he saw the sword that had been taken from him when he was captured in the hands of a Federal staff officer.[7]

"You have my sword, sir," Waggaman said.

"Are you Colonel Waggaman?" the officer asked.

"Yes."

"I wish to inform you," the officer continued, "that I have been instructed by General Hancock to return this sword to you with his compliments, in recognition of your gallantry and of the superb charge of your regiment at Malvern Hill."

Colonel Waggaman took the sword with him into the next battle in which he and Jastremski fought. It was the battle of Cedar Mountain on August 9, 1862, when their forces under Stonewall Jackson defeated one of the top corps of General Pope's army. Jastremski, however, was captured again. Two weeks later, by an exchange of prisoners of war, he was back with his regiment.

He remained with the Tenth Louisiana until May 12, 1864, when he was captured for the third time. It rained the night before he was captured and mud puddles lay like African bogs under his feet. He had no dry place to sleep the first night of his captivity except possibly on a tree limb. The following day the prisoners were led through Fredericksburg and loaded on steamers at Belle Plaine, a wharf on the Virginia side of the Potomac River. Some of them went down the river and the Chesapeake Bay on the steamer *Swan* and were transferred at Fortress Monroe, Virginia, to the steamer *Salva* for the trip to Fort Delaware. About 100 officers were taken off the *Swan* and confined to the prison camp at Point Lookout, Maryland, at the southern tip of the peninsula between the Chesapeake Bay and the Potomac River.[8]

Jastremski arrived at Fort Delaware on May 17, 1864. It is not certain which steamer brought him. The steamer *Salva* arrived there about eleven o'clock in the morning. The prisoners were unloaded, examined, and marched to the wooden barracks on the island by the 5th Maryland Infantry. The *Swan* arrived about four o'clock in the afternoon. The *Salva* was not as comfortable as the *Swan*. The prisoners on it suffered more from seasickness.

To make room for the incoming prisoners on the *Swan*, many of those who had been inside the fort were removed to the wooden barracks on the island. Rev. Isaac W. K. Handy, a political prisoner who was confined to a room over the sally port, kept a journal of his experiences during his confinement at Fort Delaware. "We are greatly surprised at the appearance of the crowd," he wrote of the prisoners who arrived in the afternoon. "A more healthy looking set of men I have not seen. They are all dirty, of course, but not ragged."[9]

Within hours of his coming to Fort Delaware Jastremski wrote a letter to his brother in Baton Rouge, Louisiana, and gave a different picture of himself than Rev. Handy did. It looked that at this time he was a tall, skinny officer with elbows sticking through his sleeves. It was Tuesday when he wrote the letter.[10] It was short because the Sunday before the commanding officer of Fort Delaware, 42-year-old General Albin F. Schoepf, prohibited any prisoner from writing more than a half-page letter. Captain Jastremski wrote the following letter and added comments in the margins because of the new regulations:

"Note"—For size of clothing—take large
I am 6 feet high—but slim

Fort Delaware, Del., May 17th 1864

John Jastremski, Esq.
Baton Rouge, La.

Dear Brother:

I am at this place a prisoner of war. I was captured in battle on the 12th of May near Spottsylvania, Va. I am entirely destitute. I have neither clothing nor money. Send me by express, if possible, immediately a sack cloth coat, a vest, and 2 pairs pants cloth also—grey or brown in color, a hat, a pair of boots No. 9, 3 shirts flannel and 3 pair drawers, some socks, woolen, a cravat. Also some money. Answer soon. Your brother,

address Capt. L. Jastremski
Co. H., 10th La. Regt.
Prisoner of war at Fort Delaware (Del.)

I have a wound in the right hand.

My love to all.

When Colonel Hoffman heard of the new mail regulations at Fort Delaware, he immediately asked General Schoepf why he changed them without the approval of the War Department. "I found it impossible to permit them to write to everybody as they please," Schoepf replied, "for the reason that four clerks in the post-office could not have read 2,000 letters a day."[11]

Probably because they could not spend as much time as before in writing letters, the prisoners were forced to find other ways to spend their leisure hours. In making their rounds of the prisoners' cells in the fort, General Schoepf, Captain Mlotkowski and other officers of the garrison found an unusually large number of prisoners paying more attention to their Bibles. Schoepf felt that the Bible-reading prisoners posed no threat to the security of the fort and withdrew his guards from the interior three days after Captain Jastremski showed up on the island in 1864.

With the guards devoting more attention to the prisoners in the wooden barracks outside the fort, Captain Mlotkowski found that his artillerymen spent more time on guard duty than in the brick casements or on the parapet of the fort. Mlotkowski himself had more contact with the prisoners. His attitude toward them was noted in accounts of some men who were confined in the fort or the sheds around it.[12]

Jastremski never referred to Captain Mlotkowski in any of his letters, but he undoubtedly received the same treatment as Rev. Handy noted in his journal. He wrote that Mlotkowski "treats the Rebels with kindness; cordially shakes hands with the Confederate officers, and admits that a prisoner not only has a right to make his escape, if not on parole, but that his duty to his government requires him to do so, if possible. His fairness, his respect for the rights of others, and his determination to recognize the goodness of human beings were exemplary."[13]

Captain Mlotkowski was, as Rev. Handy said, very popular with the Confederate prisoners. He was certainly never charged with cruelty to them. None of his artillerymen were known to strike prisoners over the head with their bayonets. Above the average mentally, he was nevertheless content with his station as captain of the artillery company and never complained that his men were used as guards. Whenever the occasion arose, however, he liked to test out his ordnance. No year passed during the war that he didn't fire 36 guns on the fourth of July.

Captain Jastremski remembered very well the salute in 1864. The sound of the Columbiads and howitzers almost shook him out of his bunk. The noise making practically signalled the efforts of General Schoepf to tighten the security of the island. On July sixth he conducted a raid of the prisoners' barracks and confiscated money, sword belts, canteens and other items. Somehow the money that Captain Jastremski had left of a remittance from his brother was not touched. As he revealed in a letter he wrote the same day to his brother:[14]

> I received your letters of the 3rd and 7th of June together with the remittance of $75 which you were kind enough to send me. I have purchased some clothing and am doing well for the present. If you could, however, send me about $25 more, it would be all that I would need this summer. Do not send it, however, unless you can spare it conveniently.
> When you answer this, let me hear of the family, of my niece, whom I would be so happy to see as I suppose she begins to speak well now. Do not forget to mention about Mrs. Keays and my sister, also of the whereabouts of Henry and Oliver.

You can write as long a letter as you think proper, provided the contents are of a private nature. Write soon. I am in good health & spirits. The treatment here is good. I am

Yours truly,
L. Jastremski

During the most trying hardships he never forgot to wish joy or happiness to his relatives in Louisiana. Typical were the following letters:[15]

Fort Delaware, Del., July 19, 1864

Dear Brother:

Ere this you will have received my letters dated 29 June, the other July 6th, acknowledging the receipt of your remittance. Hereafter it will only be from time to time that I shall need call on you for money to purchase some necessaries. When you answer this, let me know whether you received the letters which I sent you last January and April.

It has been so long a time since you heard from me that you do not know anything of my career. I was wounded on the 3rd of May 1863 at *Chancellorsville* by a fragment of shell which struck me in the throat. It has altered my voice greatly and renders it very hoarse. I was also wounded slightly in the right hand at *Gettysburg* and lastly again slightly at *Spottsylvania*. I have participated in fifteen different engagements.

Enclosed you will find a small breast pin, the work of a fellow prisoner, which you will give to my little niece as a remembrance of her uncle. Give my love to my sister and to Mrs. Keays. Hoping to hear from you soon. I remain yours truly,

L. Jastremski

P. S. Let me hear from the family in your next and do not forget my niece. I will send you my daguerrotype as soon as I can.

Baton Rouge, Aug. 6th, 1864

Dear Brother:

Yours of the 18th(sic) was received enclosing the breast pin which Ernestine appreciates a great deal. She asked me whether her uncle Leon was a little boy and if you were farther than New

Orleans & when I told her that you were a Conf. officer she wanted to know if you were dressed in blue.

The letters which you sent me in January and April were received by me but not finding an opportunity to answer you I could not write nor send money you asked for.

The family are all well. In my last I wrote you that I could not for the present send you the money you asked for, but I think that in a short time I will be able to send you fifty dollars. Be assured that so soon as I will be able I will do so with the greatest of pleasure. For I am always pleased to accomodate you & whatever I can do for you will be done cheerfully.

In my last letter I send you a photograph of my little girl which you will have received before this reaches you. Hoping this war will soon be over & that you may come home, for my home will always be yours.

I remain your brother,
John Jastremski

P. S.

I send you my photograph. Send yours in your next, if possible.

Fort Delaware, August 7th, 1864

Dear Brother:

I received your letter of the 25th of July, containing the photograph of my beloved niece. It was a source of great gratification for me to receive it. I think her very pretty. She has grown wonderfully since the time I last visited Baton Rouge. I find that she resembles my sister-in-law very much; also yourself.

I have nothing of interest to relate to you at present. I am still enjoying good health, etc. Through your kindness I have been enable to supply myself with all the articles which I previously sorely needed. Do not embarrass yourself too much to aid me. Send nothing but what you can easily spare. I shall forever feel grateful to you for your generous assistance in my most unfortunate circumstances. I shall write to you often, as you request me to do.

Give my sincere regards to Mrs. Keays and my sister, also to Oliver. Kiss my sweet little niece for me and tell her that when I return I shall bring her plenty of dolls. Send me a newspaper now and then. Hoping that Providence will hasten our early meeting. I remain,

Your devoted brother,
L. Jastremski

Other prisoners at Fort Delaware wrote that the prison conditions were bad and the daily rations of food were so small that they were fatigued after walking around the prison yard. "In my daily walks across the yards," wrote Captain Thomas Pinckney, "I would time myself to note the rate of my waning strength, the burden of my thoughts being, 'At this rate how long can I hold out?' and 'How near must the end be?' "[16]

There is not even an echo of hopelessness in Captain Jastremski's letters from Fort Delaware. He never mentions prison conditions, or food, or security in any of his letters that have come to light. With each influx of prisoners, however, the rations of food were smaller and harder to get. By the middle of the summer the prisoners spent at least half an hour twice a day in lines to the mess hall, standing in the sweltering sun and waiting for a crust of bread. Sometimes, when they had the stuff to make a beverage or a meal, they picked up old, discarded tin cans in a dumping ground, filled them partly with the brackish water in filthy ditches, and cooked strange concoctions over small fires in the shade of their barracks.

The officials of Fort Delaware never minded the various diversions that the prisoners invented to while away the time that hung so heavily on their hands.[17] They felt that prisoners who set up makeshift shops simply by stretching a blanket across a rope between two poles and made rings, pins, bracelets and other items for sale to other prisoners wouldn't have time to plan an escape. Captain Jastremski himself sent a small breast pin that one of his fellow prisoners made to his niece, Ernestine, who was born a few years before he entered the service.

As Confederate prisoners wobbled in and out of the Delaware version of Avernus, the prisoners' quarters inside the fort were occupied more by officers who had just arrived or were leaving than by P. O. W.'s who were not in the process of transfer. Captain Jastremski was at one time or another in both worlds. After being in the fort awhile, he was moved to an officers' barracks on the marshy island and found himself in the middle of a walking graveyard. In one barracks alone there were as many as 30 lame officers, several of them with but one leg, or arm, and most of them on crutches. The prisoners in the wooden barracks suffered more with diarrhea, sore-throats and poor rations than those in the fort. The wound that he suffered in the throat at Chancellorsville the year before was not helped by his confinement in a damp, unhealthy, and unsanitary building in the middle of a fly-infested and rodent-ridden meadow. Security measures in the barracks area were also tighter than they were inside the fort.[18]

Captain Jastremski felt no joy when he entered a low wooden building about 42 feet long and 23 feet wide. It had only one room, with a large cast iron stove in the center, and a row of bunks on two sides. The bunks were on three levels, the first one a few inches off the floor, the second about four feet from the floor, and the third four feet higher. All prisoners thus slept in rows, with their feet toward an aisle in the middle of the barracks. The roll was called at reveille and retreat. The prisoners had to put out their candles at 8 p. m. and keep quiet when the lights were out.

Periodically, guards inspected the barracks and enforced the rules. If everything was in order, they said "Post No. ——, all vigilant."

Nearly everything changed for Captain Jastremski when General Schoepf received an order on August 13, 1864, to send 600 Confederate officers from his bastile to Morris Island, near Charleston, South Carolina, and Major General J. G. Foster would place them under the fire of Confederate guns in retaliation for the act of Major General Sam Jones, commanding the Confederate forces in Charleston. During the siege of South Carolina's chief city Jones had placed 600 Union prisoners in a part of the city being hit by shells from the powerful Federal guns located on Morris Island.

Barely after reveille on August 15th, General Schoepf led a parade of his officers and soldiers into the officers' compound where Captain Jastremski was held.[19] The infantrymen formed a line across the prison yard. Armed with lists of prisoners, Captain George Ahl, a member of Schoepf's staff, ran his eye down each list and called out a dozen or so names from each one. Another person wrote down the names and kept tally. As officers heard their names, they walked to the left of the infantry line. Not all the others were in the prison yard. For example, Captain Pinckney, who had given up all hope of leaving Fort Delaware alive, jumped out of a window in his barracks when he heard his name. He hastened across the line. He didn't want to waste any time by going around by the door.[20]

Altogether there were 15 field officers, 22 majors, 191 captains and the rest lieutenants. Jastremski was the only prisoner among them with a Polish name. The assemblage of the officers in the sweltering sun, with the 600 officers on one side of the line and the others on the right side, reminded a witness of the Day of Judgment.[21]

At first the group was as nameless as a foundling. Each prisoner was given a number when his name was first called. Then some of its members began to refer to it simply as the "600 officers." When the group lined up every other day and then was recalled, they might have been called "the rumor roll." From each turn of events or rollcall they invented other names until eventually it became known as "The Immortal 600."

From the beginning of the group, rumors always flew, bat-like, about the barred windows of the fort, and skimmed in and out of everybody's bunk. On Wednesday, August 17, the Irish sergeant who conducted the rollcall said that they would be exchanged as fifty officers were previously when the opposing generals, Jones and Foster, quietly exchanged them in South Carolina.[22] At least one prisoner traded with one of the 600 who did not believe in the exchange or cared to go to Morris Island.

These rumors did not exhaust the energies of the 600 officers. They adopted an old French saying, "qui vive," sang, whistled, or otherwise amused themselves. Some prayed with Rev. Handy. One of them made up a ballad and sang it to the tune of "Louisiana Low Lands."[23]

In De Prison Ob Fort Delaware

1. Come listen to my ditty, 'twill while away a minit,
    and if I didn't think it, I neber would begin it.
    'Tis about a life in prison, so forward bend your head,
    And I'll tell you in a minit how dey treat de poor Confeds—

    Chorus

    In de prison ob Fort Delaware
    In de prison ob Fort Delaware.

2. Dey puts you in de barracks, de barracks in divisions,
    And den dey 'lects a captain who bosses de provisions;
    He keeps de money letters, keeps order in de room,
    And hollers like de debble when you upsets a spittoon.

3. Whoeber takes de oath dey puts him in de pen;
    Dey work him like de mischief ebery now and den,
   Dey shake him up in blankets, trow snuff in his eyes,
    And patrole him on de island, and call him 'galvanize.'
4. Where de galvanized are quartered dere libs a jolly crew,
    Dars colonels dere and majors, wid a general or two
   Dese big bugs hab some privilege, dey hab a private yard,
    Dey go just where dey pleasures, ecept outside de guard.
5. Some officers do washing, and many make de fires
    So hot on a sunny day dey ebery one expires.
   Some working gutta percha, some walking in de yard,
    And many ob de gentry lib by turning ob de card.
6. Dar's tailor shops and shoemaking, some French and German teaching
    Some scratching ob de tiger, while anodder am a preaching;
   Some are cooking up de victuals, and some are swapping clothes,
    While a crew ab jolly fellows are a gibing nigger shows.
7. Dere's anodder lot ob fellows, and cunning dogs dey are,
    Dey gets an empty barrel and den sets up a bar;
   Dey gets some vinegar and 'lasses (de whiskey am to deer),
    And mix it wid potota skins, and den dey call it beer.
8. But no matter what you're doing, one t'ing am berry sartin
    Dat ebery one am ready from prison to be startin'
   Dis werry sad reflection make eberybody griebe,
    For not a single debble knows when he's given to leabe.
9. Now, white folks, here's a moral—dar's nuffin true below;
    Dis world am but a tater patch, de debil has de hoe.
   Everyone has trouble here, you may go near and far,
    But the most unlucky debil am de prisoner of war.
            In de prison of Fort Delaware
            In de prison of Fort Delaware.

Peeping out of the narrow windows of the fort or the multi-paned windows of the wooden barracks, Jastremski saw for the last time the buildings on the marshy island, the sutler's shops, the drawbridge upon which one crossed the moat to enter the fort, the ditches in which he washed himself when he had a chance, the makeshift tents where he bought a breast pin for his four-year-old niece and other things, the sentry posts and assorted buildings. To him and the other prisoners, Fort Delaware was a crucible of bitter memories.

Of the 600 officers on the "qui vive" roll, one fourth of them had been in perhaps the most desperate engagement of the war, known as the Bloody Angle of Spottsylvania, and were captured with Jastremski. Briefly, General Lee had his well trained 50,000-man Army of Northern Virginia in a salient with the apex jutting towards Grant's center in the vicinity of Spottsylvania; they formed an acute angle. The two sides were practically locked back to back, amid the most terrific hail of lead, and for 20 hours soldiers on both sides were literally mown down like blades of grass. Among the 600 were 75 officers from Virginia, 7 from West Virginia, 40 from North Carolina, 10 from Georgia, two from Alabama, four from Mississippi, one from Tennessee, and eleven from Louisiana.[24]

Captain Jastremski took to these officers, and they to him, just as he took to the world of chivalry to which they introduced him. They were molding influences and examples. In them he found the echoes of his hopes and needs, reflections of himself, or diversion but like enough to accept him as a pious officer or sufficiently different to interest him. To survive in this company, Jastremski, the only one in the group with "ski" at the end of his name, proved that he was on an equal footing with them.

By ten o'clock Saturday morning, August 20, most of the prisoners discovered that the state of suspense was about to end. Within a few minutes the 600 officers were notified to pack their belongings and say adieu to Fort Delaware. Captain Jastremski sent John Jastremski a short letter the same day:[25]

Dear Brother:

I am one of a party of six hundred Confederate States officers who have this day been ordered to hold themselves in readiness to leave this place today. We are to be sent to Charleston, S. C., for the purpose I believe of being placed under the fire of the Confederate batteries in retaliation for an equal number of Federal officers who have been placed in the city of Charleston, and are said to be exposed to the shelling of their own guns. I am glad of this move as it will be a diversion to the monotonous life led in prison. Little danger is to be apprehended from this movement. Indeed, I am more inclined to think that it will lead to an exchange. Do not send me anything until you hear again from me.

Present my love to my sister, also to Mrs. Keays, and kiss my niece for me, etc. etc.

I shall write to you if possible as soon as I reach my destination.

Adieu,
Your devoted brother,
L. Jastremski

By eleven o'clock every officer took his place in the line and marched aboard the transport *Crescent*. Possibly because the numbers were assigned according to rank and alphabetical order, Captain Jastremski was among the first 100 prisoners on the transport.

"As the noble fellows marched out," Rev. Handy observed, "I stood at the opening of the sally-port, as near by as the guards would allow, and until the very last man disappeared from the enclosure. "Good-bye! Good-bye!" was uttered time and again, as the files moved on; and I could do nothing but return farewells, as some one or more in every rank would wave the parting salutations."[26]

5

Ordeal of Fire and Starvation

As the U. S. steam transport *Crescent* left the wharf of Fort Delaware, Captain Jastremski realized that he was the holder of a strange prize. The prisoners who boarded the 900-ton vessel looked more like beaten castaways of a European revolution than colonels, majors, captains and lieutenants of the Confederate States of America. Hardly any two were dressed alike. They wore homespuns, overalls and jeans of various colors. Very few had much of their Confederate gray uniforms. Upon their heads were straw and slouch hats, gray forage caps, some decorated with braid. They slumped down the hatchway of the *Crescent* in a wide variety of cavalry boots, infantry shoes, and sandals. Every single prisoner was carrying with him all the clothes he had in the world, a haversack or a frying pan slung over a shoulder, bits of nameless souvenirs a conventional value, a small hoard of hardtack, odd pieces of paper, and homemade sacks. There were tall, long-haired Southern mountaineers, jaunty city dwellers, and a sprinkling of foreigners.

The 600 officers were somewhat elated at first, thinking they would very soon be in Dixie, after leaving Fort Delaware, and would be exchanged as 50 field officers were a short time before,[1] but on her way from Delaware to South Carolina, with a Union gunboat joining her at the mouth of the Delaware Bay, the *Crescent,* like some obedient monster, heavy with 600 prisoners and 250 guards, conducted herself contrary to their expectations. The sunrays fell violently upon the calm Delaware and stars appeared each night like a thousand silver lamps, but a little hazy. The taciturn, 38-year-old captain of the *Crescent,* Daniel D. Latham, did not hope to see anything new in this voyage. He had worked for the U. S. Army in the same steamer for the last three years.

He had confidence in his crew. When he was not in the pilot house, he instructed his first mate, John M. Brown, and second mate, William

Baxter, who had not much knowledge of the Atlantic coastline, to keep in sight of the U. S. gunboat *Admiral*.[2]

The Confederate prisoners, packed in the lower holds, slept in four rows of bunks six feet long, 18 inches from one another in three tiers, each tier less than two feet apart. There were ports fore and aft and air holes every ten feet from stem to stern.[3] The prisoners located in the middle of the ship, near the boiler room, suffered terribly from the intense heat generated by the machinery. Captain Jastremski never imagined before this experience how men could be packed like sardines in a box between two decks. Most of them laid in their bunks day and night, and gradually became weaker, until many could scarcely climb the narrow gangway for a breath of invigorating sea air on the upper deck. They suffered from seasickness, heat prostration, and mental anxiety. The guards, on the other hand, lounged on the upper deck, talked, smoked, or stared over the rail. Their commanding officer, Captain James H. Prentiss, was from Ohio.[4]

Captain Latham bore the *Crescent* away from Fort Delaware as fast as any old steamer could go. In three days she logged nearly 600 miles. After rounding Cape Hatteras, Baxter relieved the First Mate and steered the *Cresecent* gradually westward. It was 82 degrees on deck and the wind was blowing from the southwest at 6 miles an hour. George W. Stow, who took over the wheel at midnight, warned Baxter midway through his watch that the ship was in shallow water because the wheel felt light in his hands. Baxter paid no notice to it.[5]

"The Crescent," wrote William Wing, an officer of the gunboat, in the log of the *U. S. Admiral,* "steered a more westerly course than we could in our judgment safely follow. We signallized her by firing a rocket and burning 'Coston' signals, to keep more to the southward, besides setting an example by keeping off ourselves, which she could tell by our sidelight."[6]

Despite instructions from Captain Latham to keep in sight of the gunboat, Baxter kept the prison ship on a westerly course. He lost sight of the *Admiral's* light. The ship, after scraping the ocean bottom, hit a sand bar, one bump worse than the other, and for a time Baxter, trying hard to compose his mind, was too dumbfounded to open his mouth.

The lamp wriggled in its gimbals and the ship rolled to one side. It was about three o'clock in the morning of August 24.

All at once, in the twinkling of the stars, the *Crescent* hung like a charm around the neck of the Confederate prisoners. The vessel, on a shoal about forty miles north of Charleston, but only a mile and a half from the lighthouse off Cape Romain, gave them an excellent opportunity to escape.[7] The officers wasted too much time with terms of surrender. Captain Prentiss withdrew his men, 250 strong, to the upper deck and ordered them to shoot any prisoner who tried to escape. The ship's signal of distress, an inverted flag, was hoisted, and just as the prisoners were mobilized for action, shortly after five o'clock, Captain William B. Eaton, commanding officer of the naval gunboat, saw the *Crescent* on the sand bar and came to her aid.

Captain Latham, preserving his equilibrium, was too busy with other duties to worry about the escape of Captain Jastremski and other Confederate prisoners. He cast off tons of coal to lighten the ship, moved the men on board from one end to the other, and with the aid of a hawser from one of the ships in the naval blockade and high tide, managed, after nearly seven hours, to free the *Crescent* from the sand bar.

The prison ship then headed for Port Royal, situated in the extreme southeastern corner of South Carolina where the Northern forces had gained an important base from which to operate the naval blockade of the South, to await the laying out of a new prisoners' camp. Its captain and second mate were immediately tried by a General Court Martial and found guilty of neglect of duty and other charges. The wounded and sick prisoners, in all about 40,[8] were taken off the *Crescent* and sent to a hospital at Beaufort, S. C.

On August 30, Major General J. G. Foster, the architect of a plan to place the Confederate prisoners under the enemy's fire as long as Union officers were exposed in Charleston, ordered a gunboat to escort the *Crescent* from her anchorage to a stockade on Morris Island, lying on the west side of Charleston's capacious harbor. The stockade was not completed, however, and the prisoners, guarded more rigidly than ever, were kept on the sickening transport.[9]

The longer the prisoners remained on it, the more words of woe, misery and despair were heard in the lower holds. For in its way the imprisonment on the *Crescent* was a war, not of guns and physical violence, but a war against heat, thirst, starvation, fatigue, dysentery, sorrow, darkness, and inhumanity.[10] Captain Jastremski called it a "floating purgatory."

No pen or tongue can describe the horrid sufferings, the dreadful misery, and the excruciating torments that he and other prisoners endured on the wretched ship. So fearful were the guards that the Confederates would escape in their own territory, the portholes in their quarters were closed, even when the temperature was in the 90's. None of the prisoners was permitted on the upper deck in sight of the South Carolina coastline.[11] The immense heat and absence of fresh air made their mouths fervid and their lips parched. The heat told upon their bodies.[12]

Each day that they spent in the pest hole they had less water and food to go around to 560 prisoners. Hunger, with all its biting pangs and debasing evils, ran wild among the defenseless prisoners. The mind could not for a moment regale itself upon anything else. The only thought was water to quench the thirst and food to satisfy the body. Anything else—home, family, friends, sweethearts, country, cause, liberty, self, God, or eternity—was driven from the mind. The hands and feet almost ceased to move in obedience to the will; the cheeks became pale, and the eyes sank deeper in their heads.

At one time Captain Jastremski and his brothers-in-suffering had no water for forty hours. During this time no word but water was heard. He heard the word, "water," continuously from every side and from every mouth. Many prisoners in sound health wept like sick babies for water. Their parched lips, sallow complexions, and wrinkled faces betrayed, in unmistakable lines, the depth of their suffering. One not witness to the loathsome spectacle, without amusements, letters from home, or words of consolation, can picture the shrieks of pain, the groans of anguish, the tears of affliction, and the continual wail of sorrow and torment.

When the stockade on Morris Island was completed, the *Crescent* was piloted into a channel of the Charleston archipelago, and, being fastened to a wharf, coughed up its nearly famished cargo. Several days before, the 54th Massachusetts Infantry, the first colored regiment raised in the free states with white commissioned officers, was assigned to guard the prisoners from the *Crescent*.[13] The prisoners were met by them at the wharf and marched two and a half miles up the eastern beach of Morris Island to a line of pointed pine posts, about twelve feet from the ground, which surrounded about 150 small tents.[14] Each tent was designed to hold two men, but four prisoners, sometimes three, were assigned to each one. Actually there were 560 prisoners in the tents.

The spirits of Captain Jastremski picked up noticeably after exposure to the salty sea breezes from the Atlantic. For a few nights he slept more soundly than in Captain Latham's "floating purgatory." The Negro troops hauled water into the stockade on wagons, and left it for use in tubs and barrels. They were just as careless about feeding the prisoners. They walked to each tent, cried "Get your hardtack!" and threw three crackers on the ground as if they were feeding dogs. The young captain from Louisiana wrote only one letter from there. It follows:[15]

Morris Island, S. C., Sept. 11, 1864

Dear Brother:

Together with a party of 600 Confederate officers, Prisoners of War, I arrived at this place on the 8th of the present month after a stay of 18 days on the U. S. steamer, *Crescent,* since our departure from Fort Delaware. We are encamped between what were formerly batteries Gregg and Wagner, and in full range of the Confederate batteries. Several shells burst over our encampment night before last, doing no damage however to any one. In fact, the only harm that was done us by the firing was to prevent us from sleeping for a good part of the night on account of the occasional report of the artillery.

I hope that the military authorities on both sides will reconsider this matter and exchange their prisoners in order that at least if they are to be killed by shot that it may not be caused by friendly hands. I am in good health and spirits and patiently awaiting an exchange. My love to all the family. Answer soon. Enclose stamps.

Address your brother,
Capt. L. Jastremski,
10th La. Regt.
Morris Island, South Carolina
Prisoner of War

P. S. Send me $10—no more.

Upon looking back, the letter shows that Captain Jastremski was not completely in touch with reality. He did not know the attrition of his group. He did not know of the use of the two batteries, Gregg and Wagner.[16] The firing he heard on the ninth of September was not primarily to scare him and other prisoners but was a salute to the capture of Atlanta, Georgia, by General Sherman's army.[17] By the time he wrote the letter to his brother, the exchange he expected was changed by the argument of General U. S. Grant that it was cheaper to feed Confederate prisoners than to exchange and fight them.

The day after Captain Jastremski wrote to his brother in Baton Rouge General Foster ordered the batteries on Morris Island to fire their guns into the city of Charleston every fifteen minutes and occasionally into Fort Moultrie and Fort Sumter.[18] Above all, he wanted to reply to every shot from the enemy, gun for gun, and treat the Confederate prisoners on Morris Island as Union prisoners were treated in Charleston. By placing the prisoners' pen between Fort Wagner and Battery Gregg, in direct range of the Confederate guns at Fort Moultrie, Foster gave protection to the two fortifications, enabling the delivery of supplies to them for a steady bombardment of Confederate targets.[19] If Fort Moultrie tried to hurl shells at Fort Wagner and they fell short, they might have killed some of the Confederate prisoners.

Thus day after day and night after night the prisoners watched heavy Parrott projectiles, or Foster's messengers as they were called, zooming overhead and filled their minds with horror.[20] Every shell thrown from the two batteries on the island shook the stockade like the convulsive throes of an earthquake. The misery of having their ears constantly filled with the roar of artillery and the concussion of shells, the agony of anticipating death at every moment, and the pains of hunger made them always thinking of escape.

To prevent this, the Negro soldiers acted as tough as a kennel of ferocious bulldogs. Often when they found two prisoners talking to each other they taunted them and quickly broke up any such meetings. "Look out dare, white man!" one big, thick-lipped soldier from Massachusetts liked to yell, "I's gwine to shoot! My bullet's burnin' to go into you!"[21]

Shortly after the shells from Morris Island caused a large fire in Charleston and destroyed twenty-five buildings, someone was afraid of an assault on the island and moved the prisoners to two schooner hulks in an inlet between Morris and Folly islands. As a result, many prisoners had a strong impulse to escape. Two prisoners have left accounts of how Lieutenant Dick Adams, of Farnsdale, Alabama, made a saw by putting teeth in a case knife with a nail file.[22]

Taking turns, one prisoner at a time, but six in all, among them Captain Jastremski, they used the improvised saw to cut a hole in the stern of one of the schooners, but they did not have a chance to finish it during the time they were on it. All the prisoners were ordered back to the stockade. The six conspirators were determined to escape, if possible, and hid in the hold of the schooner. They would wait until it was evening before they tried to escape.

When the rolls were called in the stockade, Colonel E. N. Hallowell, commanding officer of the 54th Massachusetts Infantry, immediately received a report from his quartermaster, John Ritchie, that six prisoners were missing. Without a moment's delay, the two officers went back to the old hulks to look for them. Eventually they caught five of the prisoners in the nude, ready to go into the water and swim to Folly Island, 100 yards away, and brought them back to the stockade. The sixth prisoner, hiding in a paddle box, disguised himself as a seaman until he was caught.

No one mentioned the six unsuccessful escapers in the days that followed, yet they were almost never left alone; one of Colonel Hallowell's men was always hovering within a few feet of them. Thus kept constantly in the regiment's eye, Captain Jastremski, more self-conscious than ever, began to examine and analyze more carefully his own thoughts and emotions.

The prison camp, in the midst of two bombarding forces, was quite different, in noise and frequency, from the battles in which he fought. When he fought in a battle, the prospect of instant death or maiming lasted only a short time and occurred in spots. On Morris Island, his ears were constantly filled with the doleful sounds of death-bearing shells, not only now and then, but every moment. Sometimes they received food packages from Confederate sympathizers, but not often enough. Both day and night, from September 12 on, there was no moment that his mind was free from the exchange of fire.

On October 21, when General Foster heard that the Union prisoners in Charleston were no longer in danger because they were moved to a safe place, he transferred the Confederate prisoners on Morris Island to Fort Pulaski, located on Cockspur Island at the mouth of the Savannah River in Georgia, 17 miles east of Savannah. The prisoners were escorted by the Negro troops from the stockade to the landing and turned over to the 157th New York Infantry led by Colonel P. P. Brown.

It is interesting to note the presence of another person of Polish descent on Morris Island and compare him with Captain Jastremski. Like Jastremski, Dr. Louis D. Radzinski, originally spelled Raczynski, assistant surgeon of the 54th Massachusetts Infantry, was the son of a Polish exile, but he was born in Geneva, Switzerland, on April 12, 1835.[23] He came with his parents to the United States in 1848 and settled in New York City. His great-grandfather, General John Raczynski, fought with the illustrious Kosciuszko in 1794 when they failed to gain the independence of Poland. A graduate of a New York medical school in 1859, Dr. Radzinski joined the Union Army, first as a Surgeon's Mate in the 36th New York Infantry and secondly as assistant surgeon in the 54th Massachusetts Infantry.[24] He joined the Massachusetts regiment on Morris Island a short time before Captain Jastremski arrived there as a prisoner of war.

When he was on duty, Dr. Radzinski visited the stockade every morning to examine the sick prisoners and give them some pills.[25] He probably met every prisoner there.

During this close though rather brief interchange Captain Jastremski undoubtedly learned very little of Dr. Radzinski's early life and antecedents. He seemed to live in a world of his own, and he hardly ever spoke of the persons he met, though he had many associations with persons from practically every walk of life.

Except for two fruitless attempts of some prisoners to escape,[26] the next five months were filled with hundreds of cases of scurvy, dysentery, chronic diarrhea, acute rheumatism, colds and other diseases which turned the bleak, dismal and damp casemates of Fort Pulaski into death traps.[27] Fort Pulaski, built in 1829-1847 and named for Casimir Pulaski, a Polish general who gave his life for American freedom in the October, 1779, siege of Savannah, was not used to keep prisoners of war before, and at first Captain Jastremski and other Confederate prisoners slept on the hay-strewn floors of the casemates.[28] Bunks were not made for them until October 26, and by that time almost every prisoner had a severe cold.[29]

There was one bright note for the Confederate prisoners in the Georgia prison camp. "Gentlemen," Colonel Brown said to them the day after their arrival, "you shall be treated humanely in my custody."[30] He permitted them to receive packages, to buy food with their own money from visiting sutlers, and to fix up their casemates any way they wished. Most of the prisoners felt that he treated them like officers.[31]

Very little is known of Captain Jastremski during this period, principally because he wrote only three letters to his brother, one of which, written in light ink, is now illegible, and the chief topic of discussion in them is money. On October 30, he wrote:[32]

> I together with the Confederate prisoners have been transferred to this place from Morris Island, S. C. I am in good health but also in a more destitute condition than I have ever been in my life. I have but one suit—a torn suit of summer clothing. In fact, I am in rags and not money enough to buy a loaf of bread. I am altogether in a wretched condition. There is no chance of exchange. Consequently I wish you would try and make an arrangement with some commercial house in New Orleans who has a branch in New York to have some money sent me in order to supply my indispensable wants. Have it arranged so that the house in New York would notify me by letter that I have a certain amount deposited to my credit for which I could make my draft upon them. That is the safest way of sending me relief. In that manner, if I was exchanged or transferred to another prison, you would not lose the money. Everything sells very high here. Try and spare me as much as you can for the above arrangement. Give my respects and love to all the family. Answer soon.

On November sixth, when he didn't get a reply to his first letter from Fort Pulaski, he wrote again to his brother:[33]

> I am at this place in good health. I have not heard from you for nearly three months. I have written three letters to you since that time. I am in great need of clothing and other necessaries. I have not money enough to purchase a loaf of bread. Indeed, I am worse

off than I have even been in my life. If you could arrange it so that a commercial house in New York would notify me by letter that I have a certain amount placed in their hands to my credit, for which amount my draft would obtain it, it would greatly relieve me and make it safe to transfer money. In case of my being exchanged the money would not be lost to you. You could arrange it that way with some house in New Orleans who has a branch in New York. Try and spare me as much as you can as I am entirely destitute and money is much needed here as everything is high. Give my love to all the family. Answer immediately.

Fort Pulaski was smaller than Fort Delaware. It suffered a great deal of damage early in the war when the heavy guns of Federal warships bore hugh gaps in her brick walls.[34] Shortly after the Confederate prisoners came there, a Union surgeon inspected Fort Pulaski and complained that it had too many prisoners.[35] Thus on November 19, when at least every fourth prisoner had scurvy, more than 200 prisoners were shipped from there to Hilton Head, leaving little more than 300, among them Captain Jastremski, at Fort Pulaski.[36]

General William T. Sherman's march through Georgia to Savannah and then northward through the Carolinas created enormous problems. Referring to one of them on Feb. 13, 1865, Major General Q. A. Gillmore, who succeeded Foster as commanding officer of the Department of the South, wrote, in a letter to Major General Henry W. Halleck, the Army's chief of staff sitting in an armchair in Washington, that he needed Fort Pulaski for the detention of spies, deserters and doubtful characters that Sherman sent him in considerable numbers and asked permission to return the vestiges of the "600 Confederate officers" to a Northern military prison.[37]

As a result, on the morning of March 4, 1865, the day Abraham Lincoln began his 2nd term as President of the United States, the 313 Confederate officers and 102 enlisted men at Fort Pulaski were taken on the 837-ton, two-masted square rigger, the *Ashland*,[38] but they did not go very far. When the ship crossed the harbor to Hilton Head Island the same day to pick up the other members of the original 600 officers, then numbering 182 officers, a surgeon complained that the *Ashland* was too small to hold them all.[39]

A larger but more inferior troop ship, the 2,123-ton *Illinois*,[40] already crowded with prisoners taken by General Sherman's army at Savannah, was nearby, and all the Confederate officers were transferred to it. The following day, which was Sunday, at least ten of the prisoners who were at Fort Pulaski with Captain Jastremski and some others took the oath of allegiance to the United States and were thus freed from the aching pains and fierce agonies of prison.

Only the jeers and hisses of the other prisoners disturbed the ceremony on the *Illinois*. With his face ashen in the graying dusk and circles of fatigue under his dark, deep-set eyes, Captain Jastremski crawled into his bunk, but he couldn't sleep. The ship with 465 officers and 167 enlisted men among its prisoners[41] reached Cape Hatteras on March seventh, Norfolk on the ninth, and left Norfolk on the eleventh with orders to return the prisoners to Fort Delaware.

Captain Jastremski wrote an account of his experiences on the *Illinois*, and picking it up at the point when the ship weighed anchor at Norfolk is memorable:[42]

> The vessel put to sea and after dark I went on the upper deck for fresh air. I was soon approached by an Irishman, who was of the crew and was a Southern sympathizer. He said to me: "They're treating you like dogs. I'd get away if I were you."
> I replied to him that I would do so if he could show me how, and that I had already made four fruitless attempts. He then told me that in the forward part of the deck, where I was quartered, I would find a hatch through which I could descend to the forepart of the hold, where the anchor chains and sail duck, ropes, etc., were stored. That if I concluded to make the attempt and would let him know, after a while—after the prisoners would be landed at Fort Delaware, the day following—he would bring me food for the trip to New York, where the transport was to go to take on supplies. That before reaching New York he would come down to supply me with clothes and to give me a few dollars. "Then," he concluded, "if you're smart, you'll be able to get back South." I thanked him and told him that I would let him know as he suggested. Thereupon, I went down for a consultation with some friends. Three of them agreed to make the attempt with me. They were: Capt. Thomas F. Perkins, 11th Tenn. Cav.; Capt. Emmett E. DePriest, 23d Va. Inf., and Lieut. Cicero M. Allen (a Louisianian), 2d Ark. Cav. We decided not to inform my

Irish friend, for fear that by some indiscretion he might have our attempt revealed. We swapped clothes with other friends, gathered some crackers and canteens of water, some matches and candles, and arranged with some of the Georgians to personify us at roll calls, and, after bidding our friends good-bye and receiving their warm wishes for our success, we went down to the designated place of concealment. We fixed places to lie in with the aid of candle light, but soon afterwards Captain Perkins, who had been suffering with flux, was violently seized with pains in the bowels and his ailment grew more pronounced, to an extent that caused us to insist upon his return to the deck above us and seek the assistance of the surgeon. The gallant fellow urged his right to risk his life in the endeavor, and that the responsibility rested wholly upon himself. We finally resolved to inform him that we could not agree to his view and that we had rather abandon the attempt than witness his increasing sufferings and danger, and that we would proceed to do so. He then consented to be assisted up the hatch. We then fell into a sleep from which we awoke by the cessation of the vessel's rolling and pitching, and the rumblings above indicating that we were at Fort Delaware and that the prisoners were being landed. For several hours we lay upon the anxious bench, but when the vessel began to move once more we felt that our absence had not been observed and that we had only to fear a telegram to search the vessel on her arrival at New York. At times during the rest of the voyage we would light the candle for an instant, eat some crackers and go back to sleep. Finally we were awakened by the firing of a cannon and soon after the ship's motion told us that we were in New York harbor. We could hear the whistles of passing crafts, and when we felt it to be afternoon, we ascended to the deck above and sought refuge there in a dark corner. After dusk one of the trio made a reconnaissance to the upper deck and reported the vessel to be fast to the pier with her stern swinging a few feet outward. We had been in the hold for more than three days and nights, and it was with joyful feelings that we emerged upon the upper deck and in turn jumped to the wharf and walked rapidly into the city. We soon crossed Broadway and hastened to go down into a cellar saloon and eating place. We called for cocktails and had a substantial meal. We were in rags and looked like tramps. Fourteen dollars in greenbacks was our aggregate wealth. We went to a cheap lodging house and got a room under assumed names. There we gazed at each other and rejoiced at being free men again. Allen had been a prisoner for fifteen months and DePriest and I ten months. It was then Sunday, March 13, 1865.

ORDEAL OF FIRE AND STARVATION

The next day we found friends who gave us clothes and money. DePriest left us to go to Baltimore, where he expected to meet friends, and Allen and myself concluded to stay a few days longer to recuperate.

As a matter of fact, while he was in the tumultuous city on the Hudson River, he wrote a letter in French to his brother in which more details of his ordeal as a prisoner of war were given. He left the *Illinois* on Tuesday night, March 14 (not Sunday, March 13). His spirits improved when he felt the sidewalks of New York under his feet day after day. Tired but happy, he felt and looked more like a fighting man after he discarded his torn clothes, gray forage cap, and nondescript shoes. On Saturday, March 25, eleven days after reaching New York, he wrote to John Jastremski:[43]

My Dear Brother:

You will be surprised to see my letter dated at New York, but you will solve the puzzle later. I will begin by giving you a history of my adventures since the last letter I received from you in the month of August, 1864. In that letter you told me you would send some money to my address (which was then Fort Delaware). That was the last time I had news from you.

So I am going to tell you my story. On August 20, 1864, an announcement was made to the prisoners at Fort Delaware that 600 of them were going to be sent to Charleston, S.C., for the purpose of being put under the fire of the Confederate batteries in retaliation for the Yankee officers who were, as they said, at that time under the fire of the Yankee batteries. I was one of this number and we embarked that day on the steamship *Crescent* to go to Charleston. They had us so crowded together that we were suffocating in the heat of that hot place from which they would allow only about 25 men to go on deck at a time. Many among us were sea-sick which increased the terrible odor that we constantly inhaled. We remained 17 days on board this veritable hell-on-earth before being disembarked.

One cannot have an idea of the torture we suffered during this time. The weather was extremely hot. When they brought us on land we were more dead than alive. We were brought to a kind of stockade which was constructed for us between two of their (Yankee) batteries which were the most advanced and which were located about 1200 yards from Fort Sumter and the other Confederate batteries. There we were guarded by a regiment of Negroes who practiced all kinds of indignities against us and threw themselves upon us for the slightest reason. Two of our comrades were hurt by these devils without the slightest pretext. They almost made us die of hunger. We received only four hardtack biscuits per day and four ounces of meat and a half pint of bean soup, and all full of revolting worms. At that time we were under the fire of our forts which in returning constant cannonades of the Yankees on Charleston, constantly dropped bombs among our tents which were entirely unprotected. It happened to me often at night to be awakened by the noise of bombs that burst above us, throwing their immense fragments on all sides among our tents. By the dictates of divine providence none of us was hit by these bombs during the six weeks of this very miserable existence.

Finally when we all began to succumb to this treatment, on October 20th they told us that the retaliation was finished and they were going to send us to Fort Pulaski where we would be well treated. In fact, we went to this fort and until January, 1865, all went well, but from that day on by an order from General Foster, they started torture in the following manner: For forty days we received as ration only ten ounces of corn meal full of worms and four ounces of bread and a half pint of *cornichons* per day. Not a bit of meat or anything else.

On the 10th day, after having eaten all the cats that we could catch in the fort, about 200 of us had an attack of scurvy.

To make matters worse, we were not allowed to receive anything from outside, but we were allowed to buy from the sutler. It is this that saved us. By a miracle the sutler was a humane man and took pity on us. He gave us food on credit on our drafts, without knowing if he would ever be paid. In accordance with this and pushed by hunger I gave him a draft on Messrs. Mioton in New Orleans for $60.00, asking them to send it to you. In this way I saved myself from the scurvy and perhaps certain death.

At that time I had dysentery which was wasting my constitution. Finally, that stopped when the Yankees saw they were going to kill us all. They gave us good rations and on March 4th they sent us, as they said, to be exchanged at Monroe Fortress.

We remained in that place two days and after that we were sent to Fort Delaware. But I was determined not to return there if it was possible. Consequently, instead of disembarking at the fort, two of my comrades and myself hid unseen in the hold of the steam ship.

After the other prisoners were put ashore, we continued to New York and arrived there on March 14th. In the shelter of the night, we jumped on land, dressed as civilians and we were free! I was free after six months of imprisonment.

You can imagine how happy I was on feeling the pavements of New York under my feet. We found friends who helped us and gave us money to take us to Havana from where we will return to the Confederacy to rejoin the army. When you receive my letter I will be far from here, for I am going to Havana at three o'clock this afternoon.

From the South in Carolina I wrote you four letters and did not receive any reply. You never saw them I think.

Pay my respects to all the family. Embrace my grand niece for me as well as my sister, Leontine, and also Mrs. Keays. I earnestly hope for the end of the war to have the happiness of being able to embrace all of you but while waiting for that day my duty compels me to fight the enemy of my country and as far as it is in my power, I will fight for the flag of the Southern cause.

Actually, Captain Jastremski did not go to Havana, Cuba. "At the end of the time we had set," he wrote in 1904, "we proceeded to Baltimore, thence to a place near Point of Rocks, on the Potomac, where we thought of entering Virginia and rejoining the Confederate forces." In Richmond, however, Jefferson Davis felt that the end had come. The city itself, Lee wrote to him on April 2, must be evacuated immediately, and was in flames by nightfall. The news reached Captain Jastremski and Lieutenant Allen probably the same day that Richmond was about to be evacuated and they felt that they would not be able to reach the Army of Northern Virginia, or what was left of it, without bumping into Grant's army. Follow the footsteps of the two Confederate escapees from the eastern bank of the Potomac River in Captain Jastremski's own words:

We decided to return to Baltimore. There our friends supplied us with funds and railroad tickets and we went on through to Louisville. Thence we took a steamer for Cairo. At Evansville cannons were being fired, as we landed, announcing the surrender at Appomattox. A Union officer was addressing a large crowd that was rejoicing over what we regarded as dreadful news. At Cairo we got aboard another boat and went down to Memphis. Finding it difficult to get out of the lines there we went back aboard, and on her trip up we were landed at Randolph, in West Tennessee, in the middle of the night. Thence we made our way safely to Meridian, Mississippi, and reported to General Taylor, whose army had retired to that place after the evacuation of Mobile. The General gave us thirty days' furlough almost on the eve of the surrender of his forces.

Then we crossed the Mississippi with the intention of joining Kirby Smith's army in the rumored continuance of the war in the Trans-Mississippi country. But before the expiration of our furloughs that officer also surrendered. The war was over.

On April 21, approximately two weeks after the surrender of Lee at Appomattox, Captain Jastremski was in the town of Grenada, situated on the eastern edge of the Mississippi Delta, and received an order at the headquarters of the North Mississippi and West Tennessee district to proceed to Meridian for his orders which, as he wrote, resulted in a month's furlough.[44]

For the war-worn veteran, a furlough was to be merely an exercise in futility. The legions of Caesar had not a more lost soul. He had been schooled for four years in privations, exposures and hardship. None of the onerous and direful experiences he had in fighting for the Southern cause effected him as much as the gloom he found in Louisiana.

In some sections almost every home bore silent but eloquent testimony to the ravages of war. He found nothing left for him in Abbeville. He could not earn there a loaf of bread, and he was too poor to buy it, too proud to beg for it, and too honest to steal it. He stopped in Baton Rouge to visit his brother and met a tearful reception. He was invited not only by his brother and family but also by his in-laws, the Keays, to make his home with them.

But unfortunately the tears of inexpressible gratitude were hardly dry before he was picked up by a company of the 93rd United States Colored Infantry and taken to Franklin, Louisiana.[45] There on June 10 he signed a form which let him live in Baton Rouge without being disturbed by Federal authorities. It read:[46]

> I, the undersigned, Prisoner of War, belonging to the Army of the Trans-Mississippi Department, having been surrendered by General E. Kirby Smith, C. S. A., Commanding said Department, to Major General E. R. S. Canby, U. S. A., Commanding Army and Division of West Mississippi, do hereby give my solemn PAROLE OF HONOR, that I will not hereafter serve in the Armies of the Confederate States, or in any military capacity whatever, against the United States of America, or render aid to the enemies of the latter, until properly exchanged in such manner as shall be mutually approved by the respective authorities.

In addition to Captain Jastremski's signature, the form, issued by the U. S. A. Provost Marshal General, was signed by Captain J. C. Murphy, 7th Louisiana Cavalry, C. S. A., and Lt. Col. Smith W. Anderson, 93rd U. S. Colored Infantry.[47] So ended the story of Captain Jastremski as a Confederate officer.

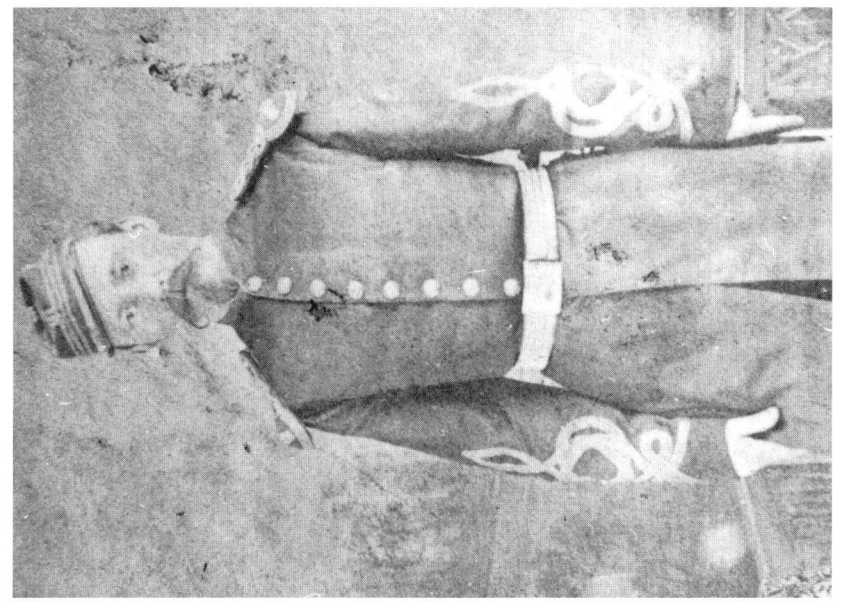

Captain of the 10th Louisiana Infantry, C. S. A.

Leon Jastremski as he appeared at the time he enlisted in Confederate Army.

Chateau of Count de Pontaut, Soulan, France, where Leon Jastremski was born.

Jastremski's home in Abbeville, Louisiana, as it looks today.

Aerial view of Fort Delaware on Pea Patch Island in the middle of the Delaware River where Leon Jastremski was confined as a prisoner of war during the Civil War.

Confederate prisoners arriving at Fort Delaware in Jastremski's day

Leon Jastremski and his three children, Eugene, Henry and Estelle.

Eugene Jastremski

Rosa Larguier, first wife of Leon Jastremski.

Estelle Jastremski

Henry Jastremski

Leon Jastremski as he looked when he was appointed consul to Callao, Peru, and autograph

Dr. Leon Jastremski, General Jastremski's nephew

John Jastremski as a young man

Ernestine Jastremski, General Jastremski's niece

Rosa Jastremski, General Jastremski's niece who married William P. Reymond in 1891.

John Jastremski in superintendent's office, Louisiana Deaf and Dumb Institute, where he was superintendent from 1884 to 1904 and where he sometimes received his brother.

House in Baton Rouge similar to one in which General Jastremski lived when he first ran for governor of Louisiana in 1904.

Sallie Land, whom Leon Jastremski married on October 12, 1881.

General Jastremski as he looked in 1900 in uniform of United Confederate Veterans.

The tombstone of General Jastremski in Old Catholic Cemetery on Main Street, Baton Rouge, Louisiana.

Sarah Jastremski Helm as a college student in 1920's.

George H. Reymond, General Jastremski's grandnephew.

Four generations (clockwise, top left) Sarah Land Jastremski Helm, Mrs. Henry Jastremski, Sarah Frances Jastremski Evans and Sarah Elizabeth Evans.

On June 9, 1974 (General Jastremski Day), officers and members of the Captain Stanislaus Mlotkowski Memorial Brigade Society, standing in front of the sally port of Fort Delaware, greeted the grandnephew of General Jastremski, George H. Reymond and his wife, Laura, from Baton Rouge, Louisiana. Left to right, Walter Maczynski, Helen Kilczewski, Jennie Maczynski, Catherine Yatkowski, Florence Nowak, treasurer, Ben Yatkowski, president, Wanda Staszczak, Laura Reymond, Debbie Tice, George H. Reymond, Jean Paruszewski, Charles Kilczewski, room chairman, Edward Skomorucha, vice president, Walter Staszczak (Captain Mlotkowski), captain of brigade, Stanley Sobocinski (Captain Jastremski), chairman of the board, and Edward Pinkowski, commissioner, Philadelphia Historical Commission. Others were inadvertently missed.

6

Proud Cavalier of Louisiana

IN 1865 the home of John Jastremski, a quaint, two-story, tree-shaded structure of French pattern, stood on Africa Street, near the corner of St. Charles, and all around it were lingering traces of the devastation and bloodshed that the war wrought in Baton Rouge. As the capital of Louisiana and of East Baton Rouge parish, Baton Rouge became an early objective of the Federal forces. Many of its citizens remembered the precarious circumstances of the city in the second year of the war when part of Admiral David G. Farragut's Union armed fleet steamed up the Mississippi River, passing in the muddy waters flatboats of burning cotton, and anchored in front of a section in which public buildings, stores, and small industries were heavily concentrated. Many merchants quickly emptied their shelves and warehouses of everything that might be of value to the invaders. An unruly mob almost laid Baton Rouge in ashes.

When Benjamin Franklin Bryan, then mayor of Baton Rouge, was called upon to surrender the city to one of the gunboat officers, he replied that the inhabitants, although "without any means of defense," would not hoist the flag of the United States over their city.[1]

As Federal officers were being rowed ashore in a small boat to hoist the flag themselves, snipers wounded and killed some of them. The Union gunboats avenged their loss by bombarding the buildings on the eastern bluff of the river. The snipers hied away, leaving the aged men, women and children of the city to take care of themselves. Many mothers, including probably Mrs. John Jastremski and her mother, Mrs. Henrietta Keays, huddled their children about them and scampered to the woods farther away from the river. When the bombardment stopped, the Union troops raised the United States flag over a public building and, after a short visit to Vicksburg, Mississippi, occupied Baton Rouge. Efforts to dislodge them on August 5, 1862, only ruined more buildings, killed more people, and caused more pillage throughout the city.

The war left deep scars in Baton Rouge. With the occupation of the city by Federal military authorities, the capital of Louisiana was moved to Opelousas, then to Alexandria, and finally to Shreveport, which was the last place over which the Confederate flag waved, and the building itself in Baton Rouge which had served as the seat of government for about thirteen years was used to confine military and political prisoners until it was gutted by fire. The Union soldiers who occupied the city were quartered in a group of white-columned barracks which dated back to the days of President James Monroe. In those days the inhabitants of the city depended principally upon sugar plantations, cotton growing, stock raising, and river transportation for a livelihood.[2] Practically all the sugar plantations, which numbered 1200 in 1861, were forced out of business during the war, owing to Federal control of the Mississippi waterways and hubs of transportation. The curtailment of markets for sugar and cotton, the chief products of the surrounding country, virtually paralyzed the economic life of Baton Rouge.

After losing the war, weary, footsore soldiers, some of them tramping hundreds of miles to return home, found gloom hanging over Baton Rouge like a somber pall. Fortunes were gone, plantations were wrecked, and many of the older mercantile firms were in financial ruin or were struggling to exist. The city was still in the grip of military authorities in June, 1865, when Leon Jastremski, with a parole in his pocket, moved in with his brother and pondered his next step.

Though he was twenty-one years old, the decision to make his home in Baton Rouge was not easy. There was everything to discourage him. Conditions were worse in Abbeville. Instead of giving up because the war left such deep scars in his life, he realized that he could not give up the struggle of life because the struggle at arms had been unsuccessful. He talked with his only brother and decided to go into business with him. He had some experience in pushing medicine pills. As the years went by, the drug store and apothecary, open to rich and poor alike, furnished the city not only with drugs and patent medicines but also perfumes, fancy articles, garden seeds, tobacco cigars, fine wines and liquor. Not long ago a local history buff found in probate records that "J. Jastremski and Bro," as the business was called, sold to Col. J. O. Fuqua a box of whiskey for $450.[3]

The name on the front of the drug store, "J. Jastremski and Bro," was a puzzle to one of the customers. Generally he heard other customers refer to either of the brothers as "Mister Jastremski." One day he caught only one brother in the store. "Mister Jastremski," he asked, "Who is Mister Bro?"[4]

As a battle-scarred defender of the Southern cause, Leon enjoyed the aura of a war hero and met a stream of new acquaintances. Among them were the South's answer to Matthew Brady, Andrew D. Lytle, who was to take pictures of the Jastremski family for more than forty years; Rev. C. Delacroix, pastor of St. Joseph's Roman Catholic Church on Main Street, who presented him with a copy of "L 'Imitation de Jesus-Christ" and wrote in French on the flyleaf, "My dear friend, Leon Jastremski, remember that God loves those who are brave;" Joseph Larguier and his brother-in-law, Eugene de la Noue, who had a hardware store since 1850; two Confederate officers, John McGrath and James Cooper, and many other merchants, physicians, and lawyers. His friendship with Major Andrew Jackson,[5] a grocer and cotton broker who was active in Washington Fire Company No. 1, may have been important in Leon's meeting his future wife, Rosa, a daughter of Elisa (nee La Noue) and Joseph Larguier, and an invitation to join the fire company. He dined regularly with his brother on Africa Street, with the Keays, and not infrequently was a dinner guest of the Jacksons or Larguiers, or some friend of the family, where he naturally satiated a hunger for social relations that had been sharply whetted by four years of denial in the armed forces.

The girl who won his heart was the bright, dainty daughter of Joseph Larguier, the hardware merchant at the corner of Florida and Lafayette streets, and a rare and perfect person.[6] She was named Adelaide Rose when she was born on August 17, 1846, but when Leon courted her, she preferred the name of Rosa.[7] No one ever used Rosa in addressing her or in talking about her. To her friends and relatives she was Rosa, never Adelaide. Leon was just as shy about his middle name. Once he used his middle initial, "J.," but he never indicated John, Joseph, or whatever it stood for. When they were married on July 1, 1867, at St. Joseph's, with Rev. C. Delacroix performing the ceremony, Rose Larguier and Leon Jastremski did not give their full names.[8]

Rosa was not greatly endowed with either face or figure, but was an angel. Small, slender, with soft, dark hair, and a small face, she retained a girlish appeal. Shy, retiring, and not too strong, she shrank from public life. Nevertheless, Leon cherished her, appreciated her wifely virtues, and loved their children dearly, the first of whom was born April 20, 1868, and named Eugene Joseph.[9] The most serious threat to their happiness was Rosa's poor health. She was a long time regaining her strength after the birth of their second child, John Henry, on August 7, 1869, and she had her sister-in-law, Leontine Jastremski, or her sister, Laura, the wife of Major Jackson, help her for several weeks at a time. Despite her declining health, however, she looked forward to delivering her third child, and on Sunday evening, December 16, 1871, Leon announced to family and friends the birth of a "fine girl"—christened Estelle Marie.

During Rosa's first pregnancy, Leon was challenged to a duel with Dr. O. Kratz. On February 10, 1868, he wrote to Dr. Kratz's seconds, David M. Callihan and Col. Ed Dubroca, that he accepted the challenge and appointed two friends, Capt. James Cooper and William Walter, to make the arrangements for mortal combat.[10] The circumstances that led to the duel "originated in the jostling of Capt. Jastremski by Dr. Kratz," who, for reasons of his own, wanted to ostracize the 24-year-old druggist. Their mutual friends, however, had enough fighting from 1861 to 1865 to satisfy them, and met with the seconds of the two potential duellists at noon the following day in Dr. Thomas J. Buffington's office to seek an agreement between them without the danger of the words, "fell in a duel," in their epitaphs. As a result, the duel was cancelled.[11]

Like many other Confederate veterans, Leon Jastremski felt the sting of retribution. At first, but only briefly, President Andrew Johnson, when he granted amnesty to leaders in secession and the war, made them feel as if they would have a voice in running the country. The military occupation of Baton Rouge ended the month after Captain Jastremski took off his Confederate uniform. But by 1867 Johnson's efforts were thwarted. Laws were passed to exclude ex-Confederates from political activity. In Louisiana, state and local governments were taken over by carpetbaggers and scalawags.[12] Under their rule Baton Rouge witnessed racial and political strife.

In spite of efforts to discourage him from taking part in the political process, Leon registered to vote on October 10, 1868, being naturalized by an act of Congress approved in 1802, and his brother, John, according to City Records, was Selectman of the First Ward in 1869, succeeding Leon's father-in-law, Joseph Larguier, who was appointed by Governor J. Madison Wells in 1865.[13] The Jastremski brothers were, of course, members of the group that actively resisted Republican and Negro rule during the years of reconstruction.

Riots between Negroes and whites broke out frequently as each sought to attain office by force. On November 7, 1870, when he voted for the first time, Leon was called upon by James E. Elam, then mayor of Baton Rouge, to quell a riot at a polling place. As foreman of Independence Fire Company No. 2 he mustered the volunteers of his company and Washington Fire Company No. 1 and marched to the scene of the rioting. Quickly, he restored order, and his men guarded the ballot boxes until the polls closed.

In that election Mayor Elam, who had held the post for three terms before the war and again from 1865 to 1868, defeated S. H. B. Schoonmaker by a vote of 397 to 274. If Jastremski had not saved the election, the Negro population, which was allowed to vote for the first time, would have given the victory to Schoonmaker.[14]

But when Leon returned from the riot scene he had no idea that his action had initiated a train of events that catapulted him from the ranks of pill pushers to the front ranks of politicians in Louisiana. The chaotic conditions of his day gave rise to new organizations, composed largely of ex-Confederate soldiers, conservatives, and prominent citizens, to fight for home rule and white control of politics.[15] In 1876, he joined a secret society called the Knights of the White Camelia, otherwise known as the Ku Klux Klan.[16] The conclave in Baton Rouge did not have more than fifty members, but it turned out in full force, for the first time in the city, together with hundreds of Democratic voters, to elect Leon Jastremski mayor of Baton Rouge in April, 1876.

As mayor he faced enormous problems occasioned by the presidential election of 1876 in which Samuel J. Tilden, frail governor of New York, was the Democratic candidate, and Rutherford B. Hayes, three times governor of Ohio, the Republican candidate. From the start, he assigned police to every political meeting to preserve peace. A few days before the election on November 7, he ordered the liquor stores to be closed during the time the polls were open, and hired about 100 extra policemen to prevent violence and intimidation at the polls.[17]

Despite the vigilance, a group of Negro voters, led by a Republican leader, paraded one night through the streets of Baton Rouge, often passing by a Democratic club, and cheered lustily for many nocturnal hours.[18] The mayor had gone to bed. The sound of fife and drum kept him awake. He had a foreboding of trouble from the rising crescendo from the direction of the parade.[19] He got up, dressed hastily and rushed to the center of town. He heard two crowds shouting at each other and then a number of pistol shots. He ordered the demonstrators, including a black deputy U. S. marshal who acted as the Republican leader, to break up the affair.

The following night, which was the Saturday preceding the election, the Democrats decided to retaliate with a parade in front of the Republican headquarters. Mayor Jastremski, however, issued a proclamation prohibiting any further processions, and the Democrats immediately said they would not parade and violate the mayor's proclamation.[20] The Republicans, however, were different. They scheduled another parade for Sunday night or the night before election. The mayor of Baton Rouge issued another proclamation calling upon the inhabitants to help him make sure that no more political demonstrations took place.

On the morning of the election, Mayor Jastremski rode on horseback from poll to poll until half past eleven. It was the custom in Louisiana at that time to have the Democratic voters enter their polling place by one door and the Republican voters by another one. He was pleased from his circuit of the polls that the custom was observed. No sooner had he hitched up his horse to a post in front of the city hall than someone told him that Democratic voters were being turned back from the poll inside Free Market Hall by a deputy U. S. marshal.

The mayor rode quickly to the polling place and ordered the police to open the door to Democratic voters and keep it and the other door for Republican voters, predominantly Negroes, open until the polls closed.

The first election returns showed that the Democrats carried Baton Rouge for Tilden by a majority of 700 votes and elected Francis Nicholls, a former Confederate general, governor of Louisiana. As a Democrat Mayor Jastremski was elated. After the election was over, he met a fellow named Clover, supervisor of the election in East Baton Rouge parish, who said to him, "You have reason to congratulate yourself that your party has carried this parish by an unexampled majority in one of the most quiet, orderly elections I have ever seen." Actually it was the most orderly election since 1866, and Democrats felt happier than they had for a decade.[21]

The euphoria that the successful campaign gave them lasted but a short time. Republican party heads in three Southern states with carpetbag governments were virtually ordered to falsify the returns in favor of Hayes. "To my utter astonishment," Jastremski told a Congressional investigating committee, "a few days afterward I heard he (Clover) returned the parish the other way, Republican."[22] Although the Democrats had a majority of over 6000 votes in Louisiana, Republican-controlled election boards in parish after parish changed the returns in favor of their candidates.

But the Democrats did not give up. From November to the following March second they fought to uphold Tilden while Republicans supported Hayes. In the meantime, Nicholls and his Republican opponent, Stephen B. Packard, were inaugurated as governor of Louisiana. The deadlock was eventually broken when agents of Hayes promised that he would withdraw Federal troops from Louisiana and recognize Nicholls, not Packard, as the legitimate governor of the state if he were given Louisiana's eight electoral votes. Similar political deals were made in South Carolina and Florida, and Hayes wound up with one electoral vote more than Tilden. It was the most disputed election in American history. Shortly after his inauguration, Hayes ordered the withdrawal of the Federal troops in Louisiana and Mayor Jastremski took pleasure in bidding farewell to the predominantly Negro troops.

The repercussion of the election hurt Jastremski's career in the future. William B. Dickey, one of the election officials who falsified the returns for Hayes, was a carpetbagger from Maine who lost his political plum in Louisiana when Governor Nicholls apparently refused to give him an appointment. Then he turned up in Washington and demanded a consulate for his services.

"In the public reception room of the White House, right in front of the reporters and others," according to a letter Thomas E. Matlack, secretary of the Abraham Lincoln Post, G. A. R., Lima, Peru, wrote to Jastremski, "Dickey addressed Hayes in a loud voice, " 'I suppose you know sir, if it had not been for me you would not have been president of the United States!' "

Dickey boasted to Matlack that he got square with Louisiana when he succeeded Jastremski as consul to Callao in 1898. According to Matlack's story, Dickey applied to the Republicans for the consulate, and upon receiving it, he said exultantly to Senator McEnery, "You fellows never would do me a good turn, so I started in for it and I'm consul to Callao now, and I've chucked out your protege Jastremski."[23]

As mayor of Baton Rouge Leon Jastremski had to deal with the problems of a city ridding itself of the evils of reconstruction. He heard complaints about racial incidents and other disorders and about inadequate police protection, street lighting, and road repairs. He signed ordinances to provide for the construction of new public facilities and to allow $35,000 for the repair of the capitol building,[24] and so on. He was re-elected in 1878 and 1880. The municipality provided aid in the care of the sick and distressed victims during the yellow fever epidemic of 1878. His greatest accomplishment as mayor was the return of the seat of Louisiana government to Baton Rouge. For his contributions to this effort, the City Council and citizens of Baton Rouge presented a handsome gold watch to him.[25]

As all political officeholders know, there was a great deal of personal abuse, too. Against the mayor's private life not much could be said; his wife, Rosa, passed away in 1873, at the age of 27, leaving him with three small children. He became preoccupied with them, but when he was sent to New Orleans as a delegate of the parish to frame a new state constitution in 1879, his youngest child, Estelle, then seven years old, missed him. On July 15, she sat down in Baton Rouge and pencilled the following letter:[26]

Dear Papa

    I wish that you were here because I have not seen you for so long. When you come I want you to bring me a locket and chain and a pair of prayer beads. We have vacation now. Have your eyes gotten well yet.

From your little girl
/s/ Estelle

With the constitutional convention in session for over three months, Jastremski had plenty of time to shop in New Orleans for Estelle's locket, mix with the delegates, learn the ins and outs of Louisiana politics, and form lasting friendships with Democratic leaders who began to come into their own. Among them were the current and two future governors of Louisiana—Francis T. Nicholls,[27] Louis A. Wiltz,[28] and Samuel D. McEnery.[29] Wiltz, who served as president of the convention, was three months younger than Jastremski and, like him, had been a Confederate officer, a prisoner of war and a mayor of a large city, New Orleans, at a comparatively young age. He was elected lieutenant-governor in 1876 on the Democratic ticket with Governor Francis T. Nicholls, and when the one-armed and one-legged Nicholls declined to be a candidate again in 1879, Wiltz was elected governor. When he died in office in 1881, McEnery succeeded him as governor and served until he was defeated by Nicholls in 1888.

    The other delegates were not uninteresting. To take just one: Judge Thomas T. Land.[30] He was born in Rutherford County, Tennessee, on December 7, 1815, the oldest son of Charles Land, a planter, and Sarah Bass. His great-grandfather, Captain John Land, was killed in one of the battles of South Carolina for American independence. He moved with his parents when he was an infant to northern Alabama and when he was fourteen years old to Yazoo County, Mississippi. He was graduated from the University of Virginia, to which he rode on horseback and spent more than a month doing it, and obtained a license to practice law in 1837. Having inherited a great deal of money, he never practiced his profession regularly until he moved to Shreveport, Louisiana, in 1846, with his wife, Mary E. Dillingham, whom he married in 1839, and the union was blessed with fourteen children. In 1854 he was elected a judge in Shreveport and four years later was elevated to the supreme court of Louisiana.

In his place as a member of the constitutional convention, the tall, erect and stately judge, with his full and luxuriant beard, which the years had bleached white, looked like Solomon in God's temple. During one of the sessions he arrived with one of his daughters, Mrs. Sallie Land Ashton, a young, pretty and vivacious widow of Major James H. Ashton,[31] and introduced her to the mayor of Baton Rouge. She was a charming talker, bright, intelligent, and a keen observer of people and events. Two years later, on October 12, 1881, the widow of a Confederate major and the ex-Confederate captain were married at the Land residence in Shreveport by Rev. Dr. William T. D. Dalzell, the venerable rector of St. Mark's Episcopal Church,[32] Jastremski being thirty-eight and Sallie thirty. She was born in Shreveport on July 14, 1851.[33]

Their honeymoon in New Orleans was brief for Jastremski felt it necessary to hurry back to Baton Rouge. Through the two or three years preceding the marriage he was an exceptionally busy man. Until that time he was usually pushing pills into a druggist's mortar or tending to his duties as mayor of Baton Rouge. He wanted to have more to say on the welfare of the state and decided to take up the pen for Louisiana's upbuilding and advancement. Early in 1879 he announced to his friends that he would launch a weekly newspaper with William A. LeSueur and solicited their help and subscriptions. The first contributor to his venture was William Garig,[34] a charitable, progressive Baton Rouge steamboat agent and businessman, who contributed one hundred dollars. The first issue of *Louisiana Capitolian* appeared on February 8, 1879.[35]

As editor of the newspaper Jastremski worked persistently to inform his readers of what was going on in the world in which he lived. He wrote most of the local stories that appeared in its pages, but on Thursday evening, September 22, 1881, just before his second marriage, he received news that shocked him and LeSueur had no choice but to write it.

Estelle, the editor's "bright, interesting and beautiful girl," LeSueur wrote, passed away at six o'clock on the "22nd instant." She was a pupil at St. Joseph's Convent[36] in Baton Rouge and was also taught by Mary Lane, a private teacher.[37]

"Obedient and respectful to her elders," LeSueur added, "she drew from them an unusual share of love and devotion; kind and affectionate to her brothers and playmates, she was beloved by them, one and all; dutiful to her father and the loving influences of relations."

How did Leon Jastremski react to the death of his youngest child? He had a chance to show it on October 31 when LeSueur's two-year-old daughter, Sadie Bird, passed away. He wrote in the newspaper:

> It was but a month ago that our friend and associate had occasion to express his warm sympathy for us upon the death of our little daughter, whose loss we felt as though our heart itself had been wrung from us. No words of consolation went farther then to calm our deep sorrow than those which were penned by that very friend who is brought closer to us today, by his misfortune, equal to that which bowed our head in grief and humble submission to the decrees of Him who doeth all things wisely. That selfishness which is inherent to man, prompts him to rebel, even against the supreme decrees of God, whenever it pleases Him to withdraw from the trials of this world those little ones whom He has elected to be angels forever around his everlasting throne.
>
> Aye, that thoughtless egotism would retain among the heart-burnings, the sorrows and temptations of the world, those loved ones, who, from the realms of never ending bliss, will watch over and guide toward a better, longer life, the parents to whom they were linked by the holiest of earthly love. When, with bended knee, stricken parents, in humble prayer, have submitted to His will, they arise armed with fortitude to withstand the vicissitudes of life, which resigned state brings the only real satisfaction that hearts that are true can ever hope to enjoy in such fleeting happiness as may be extended to them.
>
> We beg our friend, made doubly so since the same sorrows have been imposed him, manfully to bow to the unchangeable decree, as we know he can do, and by his noble example, comfort the tender hearted mother and devoted wife, by placing around her, a fresher love, cemented by a mutual sorrow, which in the sweet bye and bye will reunite them to their Sadie, the little angel, who, in heaven, prays, watches and awaits their coming.

Early in this decade of the deaths of the two girls LeSueur and a few others began to refer to the editor of the *Louisiana Capitolian* as General Jastremski. This affectionate title was in time to create a false impression for many Americans. They would forget that in actual combat during the Civil War, although he commanded briefly the 10th Louisiana Infantry, which was normally the responsibility of a colonel, the highest rank he held was captain. Governor Wiltz gave him two titles, first on February 2, 1880, when he took the oath of office as aide-de-camp to the governor, with the title of major, and on March 8, 1880, when the Third Military District of Louisiana was assigned to his command, the title of brigadier general.[38] In addition, on May 15, 1880, Governor Wiltz appointed him one of the supervisors of Louisiana State University and Agricultural and Mechanical College.[39] For the last 27 years of his life, nearly everybody referred to him as General Jastremski.

By 1882 he had considerable strength in the state because of his friendship with the men who occupied the governor's chair. With many opportunities open to him,[40] he picked, first of all, the state printing contract. He knew the members of the newly created State Printing Board.[41] By the removal of the seat of government to Baton Rouge, the job of printing law books, journals of the bicameral legislature, bills and resolutions, proclamations, court decisions, blanks and stationery, and other state documents could best be handled by nearby printers.

What the *Louisiana Capitolian* lacked in equipment to handle the potential workload the other newspaper in Baton Rouge, the *Daily Advocate,* owned by T. Sambola Jones, was able to supply. On January 4, 1882, the owners of the two newspapers agreed to merge if Jastremski were designated the state printer.[42] Ten days later Jastremski got the state printing contract[43] and every two years thereafter until 1888. Jastremski, LeSueur, and Jones each owned one-third of the stock in the new company, but when LeSueur died in 1883, the other two became sole owners.

Of far greater moment, Jastremski took his place among the influential editors of Louisiana. Merging the two newspapers under the title, *Daily Capitolian-Advocate,* as it first appeared on January 19, 1882, gave him more power to mold public opinion than he ever had before. The paper became the official journal of the State under the printing law provided for by the Constitution of 1879. Thoroughly posted in the political history of the State, a trenchant and fearless writer, he made an enviable reputation with his pen.

The following year he was elected chairman of the State Democratic Committee. He had the support of Governor McEnery, who, after completing the unexpired term of Wiltz, ran again in 1884 and was elected.

During the presidential campaign of 1884 Grover Cleveland, the Democratic candidate, visited in Louisiana and met with the first man of Polish descent in the United States who ever headed a State Democratic Committee. There were no burning political issues that divided the two major candidates. Jastremski asked Cleveland how to combat the accusations that he had slept with a young widow and that she gave birth to an illegitimate child. Cleveland replied: "Tell the truth!" Jastremski had enough time to put the scandal into proper perspective. He argued that the real issue of the election was not the private conduct of the candidates, but their personal integrity. Under Jastremski's leadership, Cleveland beat James G. Blaine, the Republican candidate, by a vote of 62,540 to 46,347 in Louisiana.

By identifying himself with the McEnery wing of the party, Jastremski lost his editorial power and political clout in 1888 when he supported the offer of a lottery company to give the debt-ridden state part of its revenue in lieu of taxes in return for an extension of its charter. McEnery was twice defeated by the anti-lottery candidate. As a result of the first defeat, Jastremski and Jones sold their interest in the publishing firm to William Garig for $12,000, and upon the expiration of the state printing contract in August, 1888, Jastremski moved with his family to New Orleans.[44] Garig appointed Jones editor of the newspaper and changed its name back to the *Daily Advocate*.

No period in Jastremski's life witnessed as much schism in the Democratic party of the state as that from the inauguration of Nicholls as governor in 1888 to the election of 1899. The four years of Nicholls were followed by eight years of Murphy J. Foster. The lottery issue was triennially raised to a feverish pitch, and the factions predicted corruption and misrule if victory should be achieved by the opposition. But upon viewing the political scene in retrospect, one is forced to the conclusion that the political acts of Nicholls and Foster were hardly worth the price of admission.

To say that Jastremski by 1888 was left in limbo would be an understatement. If Nicholls and Foster did not want to use his services on a full-time basis, he could still, with bonhommie and faithfulness, enjoy his other activities. He was beloved by all the Confederate veterans who knew him and there were very few of them who did not know him personally or by reputation. He belonged to a select and chivalrous circle in New Orleans. No city in America the size of New Orleans could boast of such a galaxy of brilliant and chivalrous men. No man who was not a gentleman in the truest and highest sense of the word could steal into the charmed circle. But any one, however poor, who was a true, chivalrous and incorruptible man, was welcome there.

He was active in the Knights of Pythias, a fraternal and benevolent society founded in 1864, and served one year as grand chancellor of the order which had about 16 lodges in Louisiana.[45] In addition to the regular lodge work, Jastremski, uniformed in full dress, especially on public occasions, sparkled like a diamond in the Pythianism of the country.

Another organization in which he was active was the National Press Association. He was one of its founders in 1885, and was elected its first vice president the following year when delegates from 21 states and territories met in Cincinnati, Ohio.[46] He headed the branch of the organization in his own state for a number of years, and probably had as much to do as anyone in the state to have a journalist accepted on the same level as a warrior, a scientist and a preacher. He advocated the training of journalists in colleges and universities as were lawyers and doctors.

For the birth of the United Confederate Veterans[47] he could take most of the credit, because prior to June 10, 1889, when it was founded in New Orleans, there were a number of Confederate veterans organizations, most of which took the name of the army in which the members served, such as the Army of Northern Virginia and the Army of Tennessee. In 1888, he was a guest at the annual encampment of the Grand Army of the Republic at Columbus, Ohio, and upon his return to New Orleans, he initiated a movement to form a similar federation of all associations of Confederate veterans. He was a key member of the committee which drafted the constitution of the organization, suggested the name of United Confederate Veterans, and nominated General John B. Gordon who became the first head of the federation. For the rest of his life he was an influential member and one year served as Major General of the Louisiana division of the U. C. V.

Nevertheless, he devoted most of his attention to the *Louisiana Review,* a weekly newspaper which first came out in New Orleans on November 28, 1888,[48] and "worked persistently with pen, tongue and hand" to make Louisiana a better place in which to live.

In size the *Louisiana Review* could not compare with the daily newspapers. It usually carried twelve pages. The front page was taken up with brief news from the various parishes of the state. The newspaper was important because of its editorials. Quite fortuitously, Jastremski had chosen the best possible medium for him to express his views. For example, he wrote, "Race conflicts are the outgrowth of the senseless experiment to have two distinct races live together contentedly on terms of political, if not social equality, between which it is extremely difficult to draw lines of demarcation."[49]

When the newspaper celebrated its first anniversary, the New Orleans *Bee*[50] noted that he had "achieved success with it as quickly in New Orleans as he had with the *Capitolian-Advocate* in Baton Rouge." "Although only a bantling in the newspaper world," observed the *Concordia Sentinel,*[51] "the Review has become one of the most influential journals in the State."

He decided when he was appointed consul in 1893 to sell the publishing firm for $2000 to his sons, Eugene and Henry.[52] Located on the second and third floors of 77 Carondelet Street, the firm had two job presses, a paper cutter, type, stands, imposing stones and furniture. His sons discontinued the newspaper but took in job work.

Throughout its brief existence Mrs. Leon Jastremski, writing under the pen name of Olive Otis, was a steady contributor to the newspaper.[53] She liked to write on social matters, women's topics and literary subjects, and translate stories from the French. Occasionally she wrote for publication long articles on places she had seen and visited.

In July, 1890, when they traveled to Chattanooga, Tennessee, for the second annual reunion of the United Confederate Veterans,[54] Mrs. Jastremski asked Leon to take her out to see Lookout Mountain on the southwestern horizon.[55] They were admiring the views from the steep, towering mountain when he said, "We better go back to the hotel before it is too dark."

"But we came expressly to see the sunset," Mrs. Jastremski replied, "and I want to stay."

"It is awful steep up that hill and the sunset will be just like a thousand others you have seen in your life."

"But I want to see this particular one," she insisted. The husband and wife, an unusual literary pair in the pantheon of Polish names, climbed higher and higher up the mountain. They paused now and then to take a rest and to exchange words. "Now," he jested each time they stopped, "look at your sunset."

7

Consul In Callao

CLEVELAND had hardly taken the oath of office as President of the United States for the second time on March 4, 1893, than the politicos of Louisiana, bankers, business leaders, editors, educators, judges, mayors of New Orleans, Baton Rouge, and Shreveport, railroad presidents, Confederate veterans and others bombarded him with letters, editorials, petitions, resolutions, personal calls, and what have you, to appoint General Jastremski as minister to Argentina. Another Louisianian, John R. G. Pitkin, who had held the diplomatic post in Buenos Aires since July, 1889, was leaving it, and they wanted "one of the most distinguished citizens of Louisiana," as Major Henry J. Hearsey, editor of the politically powerful New Orleans *Daily States,* described Jastremski, to take Pitkin's place in the richest country in South America.[1]

The fountainhead of Louisiana's strength in Washington, D. C., two men in the Senate and seven in the House, laid out a beautiful mosaic of the candidate with a Polish name and Congressman Samuel M. Robertson, a steady, dependable, unquestioning party plug from Baton Rouge, told Cleveland that the appointment of Jastremski "would harmonize the factions" of the Democratic Party in Louisiana.[2]

The City Council of Baton Rouge called him "a public servant of irreproachable patriotism, of high character and spotless integrity, a man of ability and rare good judgment, whose appointment to this responsible position would secure a faithful and competent representative."[3]

John McGrath, who ran the *Weekly Truth* in Baton Rouge, editorialized that the Confederate soldier with whom he served from Antietam to Appomattox "certainly deserves something at the hands of a Democratic administration commensurate to the long years of faithful service he has devoted to the interests of the party."[4]

Cleveland, however, gave the post of envoy extraordinary and minister plenipotentiary to the Argentine Republic to an amusement manager from Iowa, William I. Buchanan, who attracted his attention at the World's Columbian Exposition in Chicago.[5] He offered to Jastremski the consulate at Callao, Peru, which paid $3,500 a year, a $1,000 more than the consul to Buenos Aires received. On November 2 Cleveland sent Jastremski's name to the Senate, which, by action of Louisiana's Senator Donelson Caffery, confirmed his appointment the same day.[6]

On November 11, 1893, in the office of Ernest D. Craig, Commissioner of U. S. District Court in eastern Louisiana, he took the oath of office. The oath of allegiance that he took with it deserves extra attention. In 1861, at the age of seventeen, he took an oath to defend the Confederacy. Now, in 1893, at the age of fifty, he took an oath to defend the Constitution of the United States. Historians might consider it the redemption of a rebel. He signed his name after taking the following oath:[7]

"I, Leon Jastremski, of Louisiana, appointed Consul of the United States at Callao, Peru, do solemnly swear that I will support and defend the Constitution of the United States against all enemies, foreign and domestic; that I will bear true faith and allegiance to the same; that I will take obligation freely, without mental reservation or purpose of evasion; and that I will well and faithfully discharge the duties of the office on which I am about to enter. So help me God."

He bid adieux to his legion of friends in Louisiana, left New Orleans late in November for briefings with officials of the State Department in Washington, and, since no passenger ships were sailing at the time from New Orleans to Panama, he had to travel to his post via New York. He purchased a ticket for $167 on the S. S. Voy, cabin 3, and slipped out of Pier 57, New York, on December 11. It took almost a week to make the 1970-mile voyage from New York to Colon, one of the principal harbors of Panama. He spent five days in Panama waiting for a Pacific steamer that would take him to Callao. Such steamers arrived at intervals of seven days. He purchased another ticket for the last lap of his journey. In all, it cost him $250.

He arrived in Callao on the first day of 1894, and called the same day on James A. McKenzie, the American minister to Lima.[9] The land of Pizarro was then in a joyous mood, when most key government officials were out of town, and Jastremski could not present his credentials until January fifth.

During the holiday season Jastremski, McKenzie and several officers of the United States ship *Alliance* traveled over the 17,000-feet high Andes Mountains to a place called Oroya, 12,000 feet above sea level, and suffered from a malady called sorrocha, which was produced by the rarified atmosphere.

The diplomat from Louisiana rapidly adjusted himself to Callao. The illness of the consular clerk created more problems for him. He had to "scuffle with the business," as he called it, and had to learn the use of a typewriter.

At first he lived at La Punta, a favorite spot for surf bathing a mile and a quarter from Callao, going down every evening in a tram-car drawn by a mule and returning in the morning. He arose each day at dawn, took a dip into the waves which rolled in cold and crisp with foam from the Pacific, and walked briskly for an hour or two before breakfast.

"Bathing has agreed with me very much," he wrote to his brother on November 15, 1896. "Last season I took more than 70 baths and lumbage and a lot of other ills that I suffered from at home went off. This season I intend to beat the record as I want to get home in as good a trim as possible. I generally walk for nearly two hours before breakfast every morning, and I am in that respect more active than when at home. The English are great for exercising and they set the pace here."

Very few people knew details of his private life, since he kept that phase of his life to himself or expressed them only in private conversation and correspondence with friends. Mrs. Jastremski, who joined him late in February, was more inclined to discuss such things in her writings. On February 28 and March 9, however, he wrote interesting letters which were printed in the Louisiana newspapers. The first one was to Senator Caffery and the other letter was to Major H. James Hearsey, founder and editor of the *Daily States* in New Orleans.

"I am getting used to my changed situation," Jastremski wrote to Major Hearsey, "especially since the arrival of Mrs. Jastremski, who made the voyage pleasantly and safely. Thus far, she is well pleased with the climate, the people, the country, and our home arrangements.

I had moved the Consulate to a good building in a prominent place and it affords us three private rooms to live in. I purchased a little furniture. We have our meals brought up from a French restaurant next door, and have succeeded in getting a young French girl for a servant, who speaks Spanish. I am beginning to jabber Spanish enough to have my wants understood wherever I go. I hope to talk it fluently in a few months.

"The climate is simply superb and it makes this a veritable Italy of America. Just now we are enjoying delightful surf bathing. There are no mosquitoes. Fruits of every description grow the whole year and sugar cane yields as much as 9,000 pounds per acre. Coffee, tobacco, corn, vegetables, rice, wheat even in high altitudes, grow in abundance. On the west slope of the Andes it never rains. It does on the eastern slope."

Mrs. Jastremski described Callao in more detail. "I soon learned that I was living in a sort of topsy-turvy world," she wrote in a series of articles for an illustrated monthly publication, *The Logical Point,* in 1910. "The seasons were reversed and we celebrated Christmas in the summer and the Fourth of July in the winter. The greatest institution in Peru is the flat roofs of the houses, for here the servants ascend to gossip, the neighborhood cats disport themselves, and the coops for fowls are kept. Frequently my slumbers were disturbed by the crowing of cocks, the quacking of ducks and the hysterical screams of geese. There, too, was installed the flag pole from which Old Glory was flung to the breeze on Sundays and feast days, for no house of any pretensions is without its flag pole from which the flag of the owner's nationality floats on festive occasions, and a town thus adorned with hundreds of fluttering pennons is a pretty and interesting sight.

"The American Consulate was over the store of Grace and Company, the only American importing house in Callao. The first room was large and possessed two windows opening on the street, faced by two small balconies. The six other rooms were smaller, as a corridor ran along one side to afford communication. They were lighted by windows in the roof, either flat or of the elevated style called 'dormer.' There is no gazing at the idle passersby allowed, and if one pines for a sight of the blue sky—well, there is the roof—to such perfection is the Spanish idea of seclusion carried out in the construction of the private dwellings.

"Though life was dull and monotonous at the consulate, compared to life at home, yet we had our pleasures occasionally—picnics at San Lorenzo Island, afternoon tea on shipboard with the very pleasant and cultivated naval officers of visiting ships; sometimes afternoon receptions in grand style on shipboard, when a big vessel came in and the society of Lima and Callao attended in their European costumes and danced and flirted with the charming officers.

"We had a rather unique experience at the consulate, for we entertained at breakfast three United States ministers—our resident minister, the Hon. James A. McKenzie, of Kentucky, a most brilliant talker and a splendid gentleman; Governor Porter, of Tennessee, who was a minister to Chile and who was going home, and Governor Moonlight, of Dakota, who had been appointed minister to Bolivia and who was en route to his future home in La Paz. All were gentlemen of fine ability and shone in brilliant conversation and, indeed, it was a feast of reason and a most enjoyable occasion."

During his first month in Callao, Jastremski changed the site of the American consulate. The consulate he saw when he arrived was in a horrible condition.[10] It was situated in a back alley, in a decrepit building, out of sight of the wharfs, government offices, transportation facilities, and the business district, with the offices facing the sun at the busiest part of the day. Nobody could enter the small, uncomfortable offices without looking at an odd toilet, its paint peeling and often falling like potato chips on the floor and its foul odors filling the waiting room of the consulate.

The new consulate raised the dignity of the United States in the eyes of Peruvians. A 61-year-old shipping tycoon, William R. Grace, who owned the building with his brother, Michael P. Grace, made it possible for Jastremski to rent the newly carpeted, chandelier-fitted consulate at less than the government allowance for his offices in order apparently to cultivate American good will. Grace knew how to win friends. One of the 132 books that Jastremski had in an oak book case of the consulate, written by Peter Hevner in 1888, told about the spectacular rise of William R. Grace, how he ran away from his home in Queenstown, Ireland, roved about the world in his youth, started a shipping empire at Callao in the 1850's, and in 1880 became the first Roman Catholic mayor of New York City. For a third of a century, in Callao and in New York City, he sold arms to the Peruvian army, warships to its admirals, and loaned money to the Peruvian government until he was a power behind the scenes in Peru. He virtually controlled its railroads, silver mines, guano deposits, oil and mineral deposits.[11]

William R. Grace was forced, on account of his health, to leave Callao about 1860, but he left his brother to maintain his business there and eventually, in Jastremski's time, opened offices in practically every country of Latin America. Jastremski, in his offices over the store and offices of Grace Bros. & Co., noted the arrivals and departures of Grace vessels with full cargoes. Most of them were build in England and sailed under the English flag.

At first Jastremski's letters to the assistant secretaries of state in Washington were almost entirely limited to the names and tonnage of cargo vessels, but on May 11, 1896, when another company opened regular traffic between New York, Callao and other ports on the west coast of South America, he questioned the absence of American go-getters in those ports. "I would have greater satisfaction," he explained, "if I could say that the vessels sail under the Stars and Stripes and offer inducements for promotion to Americans in sea-faring pursuits by carrying American crews. But it cannot be expected of American exporters that they will disregard the rudiments of commercial science by undertaking to compete with their foreign rivals in foreign markets by chartering more expensive vessels.[12]

"German vessels bring German goods and English vessels English goods to this market. Hence the contrast of American goods coming to this market in English vessels gives rise to doubts of American manufacturers and producers to compete in anything save American specialties with their foreign rivals. I am frequently taunted with requests to explain this singularity and must confess that my wits are overtaxed to find plausible replies."

Jastremski also proposed the establishment of sample houses in all important trade centers of Latin America, conducted by American agents who could speak in Spanish and French, to promote American goods. "The Europeans," Jastremski reported to William W. Rockhill, Assistant Secretary of State, "have gained the control of the commerce of this region by having transportation lines of their own; by having houses on the ground to push the sale of their goods, and by sending commercial travelers with samples, just as our tradespeople do in our home markets."

At his Callao listening post, Jastremski attended to thousands of petty matters, from witnessing marriages to searching for next of kin and returning the personal belongings of American citizens who died in Peru. He cooperated with the American Minister in Lima and served as a funnel of important information for the American agents in Chiclayo, Mollendo, Piura, Trujillo, Tumbes, and Paita. "The posts are not easy of access," he wrote to Washington, "and no provision exists to enable me to visit them."[13] Careful and methodical, he kept accurate records of burials, inventories of deceased Americans, sales of ships, arrival and departure of ships, sanitary reports, export statistics and reported his acts fully to either the Assistant Secretary of State or Third Secretary of State.

For approximately two years, he relied on two men, John Eyre and William S. McBride, to do much of the routine work. When Eyre resigned as Vice Consul in October, 1896, Jastremski recommended the appointment of McBride, a native of Lima, to fill the vacancy. McBride, the son of Scotch immigrants, was only 15 years old when he got a job as a clerk in the American consulate and ripened into a discreet, courteous, reliable and useful assistant to the consul at Callao.[14]

"McBride has," Jastremski wrote to Rockhill on October 10, 1896, "for years performed the duties of clerk of the consulate to the entire satisfaction of my predecessors and of myself. He has a thorough knowledge of the archives, affairs and duties of the consulate. He is conversant with English and Spanish and in every way well qualified to perform consular functions."

Probably because the ships flying the American flag had to bring their papers to the U. S. Consulate upon their arrival in Callao, Jastremski led a hectic life with ship's masters and sailors in Peru. With tact and skill, he collected the back wages of sailors, found boarding houses for them to stay when they were stranded, visited those who were sick in Guadalupe Hospital, transported them to other ports, and interceded for individuals caught in situations of embarrassment, hardship, or injustice. He was an arbiter of disputes between crewmen and their captains. He was virtually a health officer when epidemic diseases existed in Peru or neighboring countries. He was all rolled into one a judge, a doctor, a statistician, a boss, and a diplomat.

He had scarcely assumed his duties in Callao when he got into the case of the Templar, a three-masted vessel owned by a group of investors with headquarters in San Francisco, and would not drop it until the laws of his country were observed.[15] The bark, built at Medford, Maine, in 1858, had left Vancouver with a cargo of lumber and a small crew.

On April 20, 1894, the ship's master, John Lee, who owned 3/16 of the American bark, reported that his Mate, J. Phillips, was taken ill during the voyage of nearly four months and had severe pains in his lower limbs. Jastremski had the Mate taken to a hospital, and visited him there several times. Phillips told him that when he shipped on the Templar he was in perfect health. He weighed 165 pounds. For over a month on the high seas he had been laid up with pains, lost weight, and wanted to go back to San Francisco.

The Consul took up his case with Captain Lee and found that, although the ship's master was willing to do it, the cost of transportation on a steamer and payment of his wages would put too much a hole in his pocketbook. Lee offered to buy his ticket and give him an order to collect his wages from the other owners in San Francisco.

Jastremski, however, pointed out that, according to a law adopted in 1884, Phillips was entitled, in addition to his wages and transportation, to one month's extra wages. Lee did not want to give the ailing Mate another fifty dollars and said that Jastremski had no right to demand it.

"My duty is to protect seamen in their rights," Jatsremski replied. "It's up to you to abide by the regulations under which you ply the seven seas. If you don't guarantee that Phillips will get what is coming to him, I have to demand cash from you to settle his account."

"Not from me," Lee retorted.

Jastremski realized that, in view of Phillip's condition, he was not in a strong position. He had a ticket to Panama and $100 in gold, enough to send the Mate of the Templar home, but he didn't know if Phillips would go back to San Francisco without a written guarantee that he would be paid there. He sent McBride to acquaint the ailing Mate with Lee's attitude. His clerk returned to the consulate with a note from

Phillips. In it he agreed to Captain Lee's terms for his discharge and Jastremski let him go home the following day.[16]

The day after landing in Callao, Lee also reported to Jastremski that he wanted to dismiss three members of the Templar's crew and asked him to conduct an investigation of his charges. The crewmen that he wanted to discharge came to the U. S. Consulate on April 22 to hear the charges against them and to present their side. The ship's master failed to appear. The case was postponed to the next day. Again Lee failed to show up. The case was put off another day. Still, no master of the Templar.

"The men have called several times on me," Jastremski wrote to Captain Lee on April 25, "and are at a loss what to do. They have not been discharged. I have, accordingly, instructed them to report aboard the Templar for duty, and I hereby warn you to provide for them."[17]

The master of the Templar showed up the following day in Jastremski's office with the ship's log book. Jastremski examined it and the charges that Lee made against the ship's 2nd Mate, G. W. Harrison, and two seamen, A. McKenzie and John Mooney, and found that when the American bark was in Vancouver four months earlier, the three crewmen refused to work on Christmas day. At the same time Lee told Jastremski that he was satisfied with the rest of the crew and intended to keep them. Jastremski decided that, as the discipline of a vessel is essential, Lee had the power to discharge the three sailors and forfeit two days of their wages.

The ship's 2nd Mate, however, claimed that the vessel was not "detained by the refusal to work." Lee did not have a full cargo when he left Vancouver and probably waited to see if he could get more stuff to carry on his chartered voyage to Callao. "Neither am I positive in my mind that the men had not the right, in part, to refuse to work on Christmas Day, which, in many states, is a legal holiday," Jastremski wrote to Edwin F. Uhl, Assistant Secretary of State, in Washington. "I gave the benefit of the doubt to discipline, but could not find any warrant in law or justice to do more than impose a forfeiture of two days' pay."

After the discharge of the three crewmen, the Templar looked like a ghost ship at a pier in Callalo until the morning of May 5. Acting on Lee's orders, Robert Barrie, the ship's tallysman who earned $15 a month similar to an ordinary seaman, forced five crewman off the Templar. They went to Jastremski for help.

Jastremski examined their articles of agreement with the shipping company and threw the papers on his rolltop desk. "You don't have any right to discharge the men in Callao," he wrote to Captain Lee. "If you break their contracts, you would be guilty of flagrant violations of U. S. law."

When the five crewmen walked back to the Templar, Lee was defiant. He would not let them stay in the Templar's forecastle. After the American consulate was closed for the weekend, he drove the sailors off the ship and forced them to seek a boarding house.

The cast of players appeared in an encore on Monday. "Captain Lee," Jastremski burst out, "what's the matter with you? Use better judgment." But that night, at about 9 o'clock, Lee boarded his vessel with two men, including a Peruvian policeman, and pulled the five sailors out of the forecastle, and "drove them ashore."

Jastremski then sent the sailors to a boarding house and notified Lee that the expenses for boarding and lodging them in Callao would be charged to him. He also called upon him to bring the ship's accounts with the five men to the consulate.

Lee took his time. What he was doing, as it was discovered later, was altering the agreements in such a way that it looked as if he could discharge the sailors at any port, upon the payment of their wages, instead of discharging them at the end of the voyage. The changes were made in violation of the laws of the United States.

When Lee finally showed up in the consulate on June 1, Jastremski examined the Templar's Official Log Book very carefully for charges against the five sailors. No specific charges were found in it against two seamen, W. Cole and Peter Grant, and charges against the other three, John Lingren, Charles Forbes and J. Heslop, were that they refused to work three hours on Christmas in 1893 when the ship was anchored at Vancouver. Lee took no action there to discharge them. He sailed with them to Callao and for the entire voyage of nearly four months noted nothing in the Official Log Book on which he could discharge them.

"Captain Lee has been exceedingly cantankerous, to say the least, in his dealings with his men and the Consulate," Jastremski reported to

Uhl. "Since May 5, Lee's actions have indicated that he did not intend to bring his vessel back to the United States, or if compelled to do so, would with a new crew that he could engage here at half the price for which he had shipped his old crew."

From April 26 to June 12, except for a Chinese cook and a carpenter, Lee illegally discharged the entire crew. He collected the money for the cargo of lumber he brought to Callao and kept it for his own use. He tried to sell the bark at auction on June 20, but the highest bid was less than the amount of his debts. Then he moved the Templar from the pier to anchorage in the bay, partly because he could not afford to hire guards to safeguard it. For some of the actors in this drama this was the last of the Templar.

The six-room consulate in the Grace building was the center of dramatic events in the months to come. There Jastremski and Lee met face to face almost daily. Each time Lee acted differently, playing a game of deceit in one act, threatening to sue Jastremski and the U. S. government in another, or trying to goad Jastremski into some act which he might use to his advantage. He presented daily claims for demurrage. One time he invited the tall, well-built Consul to a fight in the street, and when Jastremski called the police to the scene, Lee was frisked and a gun was found in his clothing. Lee continually disrupted the routine of the American consulate. His vexatious conduct grew so outrageous that the police ordered him to stay out of Jastremski's office. Jastremski finally dealt with him only in writing or through a third party.

Lee left Callao early in October when the other owners of the Templar found an agent in Lima to handle the case. The new agent made another attempt to sell the American bark at auction. No bids were made. By now everybody knew that Jastremski would hold the papers of the vessel until the wages due to her last sailors and the expenses of lodging and sending them home were paid. The amount was $620.63. The case of the Templar was closed on January 3, 1895, and when the Lima agent came to the consulate with two Spanish merchants from Mollendo, in the southern part of Peru, he transferred the ownership of the vessel to them, paid $620.63 for the return of the ship's papers, and left a sadder but wiser man.

In a report to Uhl, Jastremski wrote, "I have labored throughout this irritating controversy, patiently and conscientiously, to uphold the laws of the United States, without fear or favor, and to maintain here the dignity of the trust which the government has confided in me."

The U. S. Secretary of State found no fault with his work during the period the Templar was at Callao. The only thing he did wrong was to pay Cole, an English seaman, with American money.

"It would have taken two months to consult the Department," he told Uhl. "Meanwhile the maintenance of Cole would have amounted to more than was then required to settle his case. I took the business view of the situation and paid him off."[18]

Not all of Jastremski's time was spent on the lives and destinies of seamen. He acted as firmly on behalf of American merchants and shippers whose vessels and cargoes had no decided advantage in distance over ships from the principal European ports. In 1894, nine years before the Panama Canal was built, he advocated an inter-oceanic canal and railroad to provide new markets for American commerce from Maine and Washington to Patagonia.[19]

He estimated that the two interior lines would shorten the distance of travel for American ships as much as 3,500 miles. It would make what were then the farthest South American countries on the Pacific the nearest to the United States. He reported to Assistant Secretary of State Uhl:

"A vast and increasing population in the United States, whose industries yield a profusion of products from the fields, the mines and the factories, largely exceeding the home demands, cannot with wisdom and safety be circumscribed, comparatively speaking, in their commercial operations, to their own territory. It would seem judicious to establish these interior lines, against which it would be physically impossible for the European nations to compete, and throw open, as they would, to the wonderful American activity which has transformed our Great West, from a desert into thriving and powerful States, the continent of South America."

From time to time Jastremski escaped official burdens by going to see the massive ruins of Cuzco, Pizarro's tomb and the portrait of St. Rose of Lima in two of Lima's shrines, and bullfights at the Plaza de Acho, where most of the world's best matadors have appeared. In the summer of 1894 he visited the largest sugar hacienda in Central Peru, observed its methods of operation and labor system, and gathered "thoroughly reliable data" to enable American sugar planters to compare the sugar industries of the two countries.[20]

In order to help the American farmers, he arranged to have ten varieties of giant corn, produced in and around Cuzco, sent to the Department of Agriculture in Washington and to the Louisiana Experiment Station in Baton Rouge. From Callao in the spring of 1895 he sent more than 200 pounds of samples to various farming centers.[21]

As the representative of a foreign state, Jastremski kept a watchful eye on two rival candidates for the presidency of Peru. General Andres Caceres, who rose to power in 1885, lost many of his supporters in the ring of mountains around Lima to Nicolas De Pierola, a nervous, romantic, imprisoned antagonist.[22] Pierola formed a coalition of Civilists and Democrats and on March 16, 1895, organized a revolution which, in a desperate three-day battle in Lima and minor riots elsewhere, toppled the regime of Caceres.

Of deep concern to Jastremski was the protection of American lives and property in Callao. There were no American warships in Peruvian waters. McKenzie was hemmed in with the rest of the Limenos, and Jastremski decided, in view of existing conditions, to send a dispatch with a graphic picture of the riots to Assistant Secretary of State Uhl by means of a sea captain on his way to Panama and to do what he could by his own wits.[23]

No sooner had he written his report than a train arrived in Callao with news that fighting had stopped in Lima. The next day, March 22, Jastremski went to Lima to see McKenzie. The streets of Lima were littered with bodies. Windows were broken, houses honeycombed with bullet holes, many of them burned to the ground, and the street in front of the U. S. legation closed by a barricade.[24]

Jastremski somehow got into the legation and consulted with McKenzie about the next step they would take. He reported to Uhl: "He instructed me on the arrival of the U. S. revenue steamer 'Commodore Perry,' to request her Captain to come with me to see him. This vessel did not reach anchorage till the morning of the 24th. At that time, matters were still in an unsettled condition. Callao was filled with disbanded

Cacerist troops, while Gen. Caceres was aboard the French warship, 'Duchaffault,' which was in the harbor. Some nights before, an attempt had been made to set fire to the store of W. R. Grace & Co., over which is the Consulate."[25]

As soon as the revenue cutter anchored, Captain H. D. Smith sent an officer in a gig to pick up Jastremski. Captain Smith described what happened next: "He came off in great excitement, saying that American interests were in danger, and that Americans were liable to lose their lives unless some protection was afforded them. He told me of the attempt to burn the American legation at Lima. I immediately detailed officers, twenty-five men and a rapid-firing gun with thirty rounds of ammunition, to aid Gen. Jastremski whenever circumstances should require. The force was held in readiness to disembark at a moment's notice."[26]

Shortly after, Captain Smith, Lieutenant Johnson and Jastremski went to Lima for a conference with the American Minister. "The walls of the American legation were pierced," Captain Smith later said. "Mrs. McKenzie had been standing near the window looking out when her husband called her away and as she turned a shot passed the spot where she had been standing."[27]

McKenzie requested Smith to keep the American cutter at Callao till further developments. "Happily, the situation improved with every succeeding day," said Jastremski. On the evening of March 28, McKenzie notified Captain Smith that, in his judgment, the provisional government was established firmly enough to prevent further outbreaks and saw no reason to detain him. Both McKenzie and Jastremski wrote letters of thanks[28] to Captain Smith for the protection afforded the legation in Lima and the consulate in Callao and, accordingly, the little American cutter left the harbor in the forenoon of the 29th.

The newspapers of Louisiana soon focused public attention upon Jastremski's efforts to save the lives of Americans in Peru. The publicity sparked his friends to present his name to President Cleveland and have him appointed Consul-General at Havana to succeed Ramon Williams who had just been recalled as *persona non grata.* The first newspaper to support the appointment was *The Daily Advocate,* [29] official organ of the State, in Baton Rouge, and another strong supporter was *The Times-Democrat,*[30] official organ of the city of New Orleans. "Gen. Jastremski," said *The Daily States,* May 15, 1895, "is eminently qualified to fill the position with honor and credit." *Shreveport Times* stated,[31] "No man would more admirably, more firmly, more satisfactorily fill that important mission."

To go back to Callao, Jastremski enjoyed the hospitality of distinguished English-speaking inhabitants in and out of his line of service. Unexpectedly, in the spring and summer of 1896, he found himself involved in a religious dispute. From the beginning of his mission, he served as a trustee of a spacious, one-story wooden church on Calle del Teatro, one of the principal streets of Callao, donated for the religious and educational purposes of the local English-speaking Protestants.[32] The other two trustees were the consul of Great Britain in Callao and the manager of a steamship line. Afterwards he recalled that Captain William Wheelwright, founder of the Pacific Steam Navigation Company, had the wood brought from his hometown of Newburyport, Massachusetts, to build the one story edifice.

Unlike most of the English-speaking inhabitants, Jastremski was a Roman Catholic and felt little urgency to go to the Protestant church when Catholic masses were close at hand. When, however, at the request of Rev. J. M. Spangler, an American Methodist clergyman, he tried to negotiate with other trustees and church officials for the right of Rev. Spangler to use the Protestant church building when it was unoccupied, he was seen more often at meetings and divine services in the wooden church—in vain, as it turned out. He was ruled out of order at meetings. His wife, Sally, a Protestant from Shreveport, La., was unable to rent a pew in the Protestant church. The church officers held that the property was only for Anglicans, members of the Anglican Church of England, and Anglo-American friendship, as far as Jastremski was concerned, suffered.

After failing to convince the Anglicans that the church was built for English-speaking Protestants of various sects, he protested to William W. Rockhill, Assistant Secretary of State. "The wood that shelters the worshippers of this church," he wrote, "comes from a land where religious toleration and liberty of conscience are cardinal principles in the laws, and the narrow and exclusive spirit of sectarian bigotry should find no place under the hospitable rafters of this church." Though a Presbyterian, Minister McKenzie, a pewholder for three years in the Anglican Church of Lima, gave up his pew in protest when Jastremski told him of the steps he had taken to vindicate the rights of an American clergyman.

The 28th presidential election of the United States in 1896 forced Jastremski to think of his personal affairs. William McKinley, a Republican candidate with a lavish campaign fund, won the election. On February 18, 1897, about two weeks before McKinley began his first term, Jastremski applied to Rockhill for a two months' leave of absence, but the Assistant Secretary of State never acted on it.[33] After a month of silence, U. S. Senator Samuel D. McEnery, who began his term at the same time as McKinley, went to the State Department to inquire about his friend's leave of absence. Rockhill could not find the original application. McEnery then made a new one, without Jastremski's knowledge, and Rockhill granted it. Jastremski did not know that he could take a leave of absence until he got McEnery's letter on April 12. He was not entirely satisfied. He needed official notification so he could get a good steamer connection.[34]

He wired to Rockhill, "Is my leave mailed,"[35] and at 3 o'clock in the afternoon of the same day he received Rockhill's reply, "Yes."

After an absence of three years, Jastremski returned to New Orleans on May 7, spending 25 days in transit,[36] and he met his two sons, Eugene and Henry, who remained in Louisiana while he was away with his wife.[37] He left the American consulate in Callao in the capable hands of McBride.

During his vacation in New Orleans he read in the newspapers that McKinley appointed someone else to serve as American consul in Callao. On July 3, he wrote to William R. Day, new Assistant Secretary of State,[38] and asked him what to do. The reply closed his diplomatic career.

Of all the correspondence he received during his diplomatic career, the one he treasured the most was the letter from Senator Caffery on April 23, 1894, when he referred to a conversation with President Grover Cleveland:

"I saw the President very recently, and he expressed to me his gratification at the able manner in which you are discharging your functions, and said he considered you the best consul in South America. This was as pleasing to me as I know it must be to you."[39]

8

The Last Campaign

BY the turn of the century Leon Jastremski had become more portly, his hair had thinned and turned white, his broad face had grown fleshier and somewhat more rubicund, yet his energy was good for a man nearing his sixties. If his appearance had changed over the years, his manner was still genial and to some, perhaps, jovial. Col. T. Sambola Jones, who was his partner for a number of years and co-editor of the *Capitolian-Advocate,* once called him "as gentle as a woman until aroused, and then cool, but the soul of courage."[1] Courtly and polite, the bearer of an ancient Polish name looked to younger men like a handsome Civil War veteran with a white walrus mustache.

Upon leaving Callao, Peru, he didn't know what he was going to do. Another diplomatic post might be offered to him. With a Republican in the White House, a Union veteran of the Civil War by the name of William McKinley, the chances were slim. A well-informed man, he found time to discuss the issues of the day. He was an enthusiast for the business development of the South, and when he was not able to pursue a diplomatic career, he was appointed commissioner of the Louisiana State Board of Agriculture and Immigration.

On February 24, 1898, he presented a skillful review of the advantages of New Orleans and Louisiana for commerce with South America to the New Orleans Chamber of Commerce,[2] and contributed, in his new position, to the growth of Louisiana by attracting new settlers and opening more land for farming.

The position was not permanent, and upon leaving it he moved to Shreveport, second in size among Louisiana cities, lying on the west bank of the Red River, in the northwestern corner of the State. He started a new paper called the *Shreveport Outlook*. He and his wife lived in the Morris House, conducted by Mrs. Kate C. Bailey at 324 Market Street, while his youngest son, Eugene, who handled the clerical duties of the newspaper, stayed at the City Hotel on Milam Street. The office of the *Shreveport Outlook* was at 203 Milam Street, six doors from the hotel where Eugene stayed. The three did not live in Shreveport very long.[3]

When William Wright Heard was elected Governor of Louisiana in 1900, Leon Jastremski returned to Baton Rouge to serve as Heard's private secretary. He obtained a clerk's job in the state house for Eugene. His other son, Henry, was Secretary of the Louisiana Deaf and Dumb Institute.[4] All of them were active in politics.

Louisiana was perennially in political trouble and Heard was the first governor whose power was not as strong as that of former governors who reigned under the constitution that Jastremski helped to adopt in 1879. The state adopted a new constitution in 1898 which established property and educational qualifications for voters, restored the powers of the legislature and decreased the power of the governor. It established the one party system which has since prevailed in the state's politics.

The political conditions of Louisiana irritated Jastremski.[5] He thought that state politics needed a radical change, not the change made in 1898. Under the old constitution the governor had a better chance to lead the populace by pandering to their prejudices and passions. As a staunch Democrat and loyal Louisianian, Jastremski knew a succession of governors and leaders of the state assembly. In 1903, when he attended a gathering of Confederate veterans in New Orleans, he talked so convincingly about his political opinions that the men with whom he served in the battles of Fredericksburg, Sharpsburg, Gettysburg, and the Wilderness encouraged him to enter the race for Louisiana's highest political office.

He agreed to run for Governor of Louisiana on a reform platform. He resigned as Heard's private secretary and prepared to canvass Louisiana's 59 parishes for political support. With an area of 48,506 square miles, the state, shaped like a boot, with the toe pointing eastward, was larger than New York, and more difficult to cover from the coastal marshes in the south to the pine hills and bluffs in the northern part of the state. He created considerable surprise in the Pelican State when he announced his candidacy for governor.

The political leaders of a few parishes thought the announcement was a joke. A former U. S. Congressman and Senator, 54-year-old Newton

C. Blanchard, resigned as associate justice of the Supreme Court of Louisiana in 1903 to run as the candidate of the Democratic committee.[6]

Jastremski had an uphill fight. Blanchard began with the party machinery in his favor. Jastremski's campaign aroused the voters of the state, but he failed to cut down Blanchard's majority enough to win the election. He showed unusual strength for an independent candidate. "There were many who stated afterwards," reported a Baton Rouge newspaper, "that if the campaign had continued much longer he would have been elected."[7] Blanchard was Governor of Louisiana from 1904 to 1908.

After his defeat General Jastremski established another weekly newspaper, which he called *The People,* and made it serve the double purpose of earning enough to give him a bare subsistence and expressing his opinions on political issues.[8] The newspaper came out on Saturdays and the first issue appeared on April 23, 1904.[9] The office of the newspaper was located at 307 Florida Street,[10] not far from the old State Capitol, and contained very little furniture, including an office desk, a rocking chair, an arm chair, and half a dozen other assorted chairs. The printing equipment included a composing stone, type, and a calligraph machine.[11]

His two sons lost their political jobs when Blanchard took office. Eugene then worked on *The People* and lived at one time at 212 Florida Street. Henry found a job as bookkeeper and cashier with the Garig-Wilson Company, and lived with his father and step-mother at 415 Laurel Street for a year or two.[12] In 1905 Henry, the most educated of the two sons, married Frances Holloway, of Georgetown, Kentucky,[13] and two years later, on November 16, 1907, they had a daughter,[14] whom they named Sarah Land, after General Jastremski's second wife.

All of Jastremski's three children by his first wife were born in Baton Rouge. The third child, Estelle, died as a little girl. He kept pace with John Jastremski, who had four children by Leontine Keays, and when the two brothers paid each other occasional visits they talked about their children as well as politics, philosophy, and other subjects. To those who are interested in genealogies, it would not be out of place to give such information at this point and show the names of kinfolk he had to keep in his mind in his peregrinations about Louisiana.[15]

Unlike the General's two sons, John Jastremski did not get fired when administrations changed in Baton Rouge. He was superintendent of the Louisiana Institute for the Education of the Deaf and Dumb and Blind at Baton Rouge from August 13, 1884 until his death on July 5, 1904.

His four children had spent most of their youth in the Deaf and Dumb Institute. The oldest child, Ernestine Marie,[16] who was born April 17, 1860, and the other girl, Rosa Henrietta,[17] who was born August 15, 1867, were educated in St. Vincent's Young Ladies Academy at Cape Girardeau, Missouri, Rosa being valedictorian of her class. Ernestine taught the deaf in her father's institute.

The wedding of Rosa Henrietta took place in the institute on July 8, 1891, when she married William P. Reymond, son of D. F. and Henrietta (nee Isett) Reymond, of Baton Rouge. They had seven children: 1. John Joseph,[18] born August 14, 1892; 2. Etta, born October 16, 1893, died November 5, 1900; 3. William Phillips, Jr.,[19] born April 23, 1895; 4. George Hebb,[20] born November 20, 1898; 5. James Bernard,[21] July 21, 1900; 6. Mary Leontine,[22] June 1, 1902; 7. Leon Jastremski,[23] June 22, 1909. The Reymonds engaged a teacher by the name of Nina Martinez to open a private school in their home, and after she was finished with them six of them went to Louisiana State University and earned Bachelor's degrees.

The oldest son of John and Leontine Jastremski was born October 2, 1864, in Baton Rouge and they named him Leon after the Confederate soldier.[24] He received his literary education at the U. S. Naval Academy at Annapolis, Maryland, and when he returned to Baton Rouge in 1884, he was employed as business manager of the *Capitolian-Advocate,* the official organ of the state, with which his uncle was connected. He spent two years on the newspaper, and then entered the medical school of Tulane University. After he was graduated in 1888, he worked one year at the state quarantine station at the mouth of the Mississippi River and then established a medical practice with Dr. C. A. Duval in Houma, the seat of Terrebonne Parish, in southern Louisiana. Dr. Duval, a descendant of Huguenots who had been close friends of Thomas Jefferson in Virginia, came to Houma almost directly from the Confederate Army in which he had served as a surgeon of the 26th Louisiana Infantry. He was married to Julia Easton in 1860. Their only daughter, Gwinette Duval, married Dr. Leon Henry Jastremski on February 6, 1893, in

St. Matthew's Episcopal Church, Houma. Three of their six children were the last male heirs of the Jastremski name; Leon Jastremski died Jan. 8, 1931, without issue; John Duval Jastremski died August 12, 1957, and Stanwood Duval Jastremski, May 30, 1968, each having no male issue. The other three children were Julia (Mrs. Patrick L. Higgins), Gwinette (Mrs. Carl E. Lewis), and Margaret, who died as an infant.

The youngest son of John and Leontine Jastremski was named Vincent after his father.[25] He was born July 17, 1878. He was sent to St. Stanislaus College at Bay St. Louis, Mississippi, and the medical school of Tulane University. He started a medical practice in Montegut, a village eight miles southeast of Houma, and was not married until late in life. He married Mrs. Blanche Savoy of Church Point, Louisiana.

The joys and sorrows of the Jastremski clan were many. In his last years, when graduations, weddings, christenings, and deaths came with increasing frequency, there were many gatherings of the clan. Little is preserved of the places of receptions. Stopping six months in this place and a summer in that, Leon Jastremski had the least permanent address of them all. Within a short time the house he occupied with his second wife and Henry on Laurel Street was given up in favor of a small bungalow at 413 St. Hypolite Street, and Henry and his new bride moved to 112 8th Street. Whatever changes took place, the family circle remained as closely knit as ever. Most of them lived not far apart, kept all family anniversaries together, and shared a long list of institutional interests. Proud of his Polish heritage and faith, the General was a loyal adherent of the Catholic Church.

In between family gatherings Leon Jastremski had enough time to pay attention to the approaching election for governor. Some political leaders expected him to run again. Early in 1907 Jared Y. Sanders, Lieutenant Governor of Louisiana, assumed that he was heir apparent to Governor Blanchard and was the first candidate to announce his candidacy. He said that he would adopt practically the same platform that Jastremski came up with in 1903 and espoused in his newspaper continually since then. Owing to a severe illness which confined him to his home for months, Jastremski did not announce he was a candidate until June, 1907.[26]

The voters of Louisiana saw little difference in the position of the two leading candidates on the Democratic ticket. Jastremski, however, was physically changed in his second campaign for governor. When he appeared on the hustings he did not look the same as in 1903. His physical appearance was greatly altered.

As a reporter of the *Daily State* described him, "A man of wonderfully fine physique, over six feet tall and massive in his proportions, he was now thin and emaciated, and while his eyes still flashed the old fire, it was apparent to all that he could not stand the exertion of a grueling campaign. He made a few speeches and was given a cordial greeting by his followers, but they saw that he was not the same man, and frequent doubts were expressed of his ability to remain in the fight."[27]

He continued to campaign, though persons he had counted to help him were beginning to leave him. Old age and illness weighed upon him.

"Don't tell me if I'm in danger!" he told Dr. Louis F. Reynaud, his family doctor. "I don't want to be hindered in my fight!"[28]

On November 20, he was stricken with paralysis, and for little more than a week lay at death's door. His opponent, Lieutenant Governor Sanders, paused during the unveiling of a bronze and stone Confederate monument in Plaquemine, a town across the Mississippi River from Baton Rouge, but a few miles farther down, to refer to Jastremski's illness.

"I cannot refrain upon this occasion from expressing the thought which I know is uppermost in each of your minds," he said, "that the angel of death who passed General Jastremski on many a bloody battlefield, in the war between the states, will spare him to his family, friends, and state for many a year to come. When I express the hope that that brave and chivalrous Confederate soldier, who so lately stricken almost unto death in the city of Baton Rouge, may soon recover I know that it is also your hope that that gallant gentleman may from his bed of pain and illness arise. . . .

"The feelings of all this audience I know only express in saying that our hearts go out to him and his, and we join our prayers with those who have kept steady watch and ward at his bedside, that he may in this desperate battle with death prove the victor."[29]

He was cared for by his wife, Sally Land, and his sons, Eugene and

Henry, and was examined more frequently by Dr. Reynaud. When the faithful physician left the General's bedside at 11 o'clock on the evening of November 28, less than two weeks after Henry's wife delivered his first and only grandchild, he told the members of the family that the end was near for the gallant soldier. Three hours and five minutes later he was dead.

No sooner had the news of his death been sent across the telegraph wires than messages came to his family from throughout the country. Honesty, fairness, gentleness, reverence and respect for women were the qualities on which his friends most dwelt. The flags of Baton Rouge were lowered to half mast. The business offices of the city and state were closed for his funeral.

Wade H. Bynum, Mayor of Baton Rouge, issued the following proclamation:

"The untimely death of General Jastremski in the midst of his active life and great usefulness as a public citizen calls to the mind of every true and loyal citizen of our city not only his blameless and exalted life for so many years at this, his home, but more particularly his conspicuous service covering so many years of his activity.

"He was a gallant Confederate soldier who won laurels for us upon the field of battle.

"He represented this city in the Constitutional Convention of 1879 and it was largely through his great devotion and splendid services that Louisiana's capital was returned to our city.

"For six years, probably the most troublous period in our city's history, he was its chief executive, conducting its affairs with wisdom, intelligence and great devotion to its interests.

"At the time of his death he stood prominent in Louisiana as a leader and exponent of what is best in public life. Mindful, therefore, of his public services and private virtues, it should be, and is, the pride of every Baton Rougean to do honor to his name and memory. Therefore, I, Wade H. Bynum, Mayor of the city of Baton Rouge, have seen fit to issue this, my proclamation, calling upon all citizens to suspend their labors and close their places of business during the hour of the funeral ceremonies of this distinguished Louisianaian, and thus pay tribute to him who has been our faithful servant in war and peace."[30]

Baton Rouge's City Council met in a special session at noon of the same day and adopted a similar resolution. The Senate of Louisiana paused to pay tributes to him. "I have known General Jastremski all my life," said one senator, "and there was no man whom I respected more or who was more beloved."[31]

Governor Blanchard said: "I was greatly grieved to hear of the death of General Jastremski. His death will be a great loss to the State, of which he was a patriotic and useful citizen. General Jastremski took a prominent part in the civic affairs of Louisiana and in all the duties of public life he was actuated by high motives and noble impulses. He was a conspicuous figure in the part Louisiana took in the struggle between the States and earned in that conflict an enduring reputation for courage and patriotism."[32]

The most appropriate tributes, however, were the editorials in various newspapers.[33] The *Daily State* carried on the day of his death, "Faithful unto Death," and a few chosen extracts from it will enable the reader to gauge the influence that Jastremski had in Louisiana:[34]

> "Louisiana has lost an adopted son whose life, and works, and ending will serve for inspiration so long as her history runs.
>
> "Of heroic blood, his life was equal to his lineage. As his father sacrificed fortune and home and kindred for the liberty of Poland, so the son in his youth offered his body for his adopted motherland and in his old age went on to certain death rather than give up a fight for principle he deemed vital.
>
> "Younger men, stronger men, men who had opposed him in the past, had become converts to his ideas, had occupied the ground he held before and were perhaps to be the gainers in place and prestige by fighting under the banners that were once his—but he, disdaining compromise, had gone on ahead, had seized new ground far in advance, too far in advance mayhap, of the thronging multitude and the doubtful people.
>
> "No man who knew him but was convinced that it was the principle and the sense of duty and but little of the lust of office which spurred him on. He had lived too long not to know the hollowness of public office, too long not to know how often feet of clay hinder the progress of those in high place and how high place exposes every weakness.
>
> "But he had lived long enough, was born of a generation heroic enough to grasp in its eternal verity that the thing to do and the

spirit of the doing are the two essentials, are the two indices of character and of life.

"Louisiana owes most of all she is today to the generation of which General Leon Jastremski was such a splendid example—and while the younger men may carry her on to a future of which the veterans of the past have never dared to dream, when the story of the State is told, to the splendid citizen of Baton Rouge will be given the credit for rousing the commonwealth to her freer, cleaner, nobler life political of today.

"Ever faithful in life, he was 'Faithful unto Death!' "

The funeral of General Jastremski was held at 10:30 a.m. on November 30 from the family residence on Main Street, near St. Anthony Street, and church services were conducted in St. Joseph's Catholic Church. The route was lined by people of Baton Rouge, out by the thousands to pay their respects, as had hundreds of friends and dignitaries, and interment took place in the seventh row of graves in the shadow of the Catholic Church, approximately 100 feet from Main Street.

According to his wish, the last son of a Polish exile was buried in the suit he had worn for the past several years at the different Confederate reunions in Louisiana, the gray of the soldiers of the South.

"JASTREMSKI" is carved in the white marble saddle at the front of the family plot.[35] In addition to General Jastremski, the plot contains the bodies of his first wife, Rosa, his brother and his wife and daughter Ernestine. The marker on his grave is inscribed:

LEON JASTREMSKI
BORN AT SOULAN, FRANCE, JULY 17TH, 1843
DIED AT BATON ROUGE, LA., NOV. 29TH, 1907
CAPTAIN 10TH LA. REGIMENT C. S. A.
MAYOR OF BATON ROUGE 1876–1881
MEMBER OF CONSTITUTIONAL CONVENTION 1879
PRESIDENT LA. PRESS ASSOCIATION
BRIGADIER GENERAL LA. STATE NATIONAL GUARD
STATE PRINTER 1882–1888
MAJOR GENERAL UNITED CONFEDERATE VETERANS
U. S. CONSUL OF PERU 1893–1897
COMMISSIONER OF AGRICULTURE AND IMMIGRATION 1899–1900

***

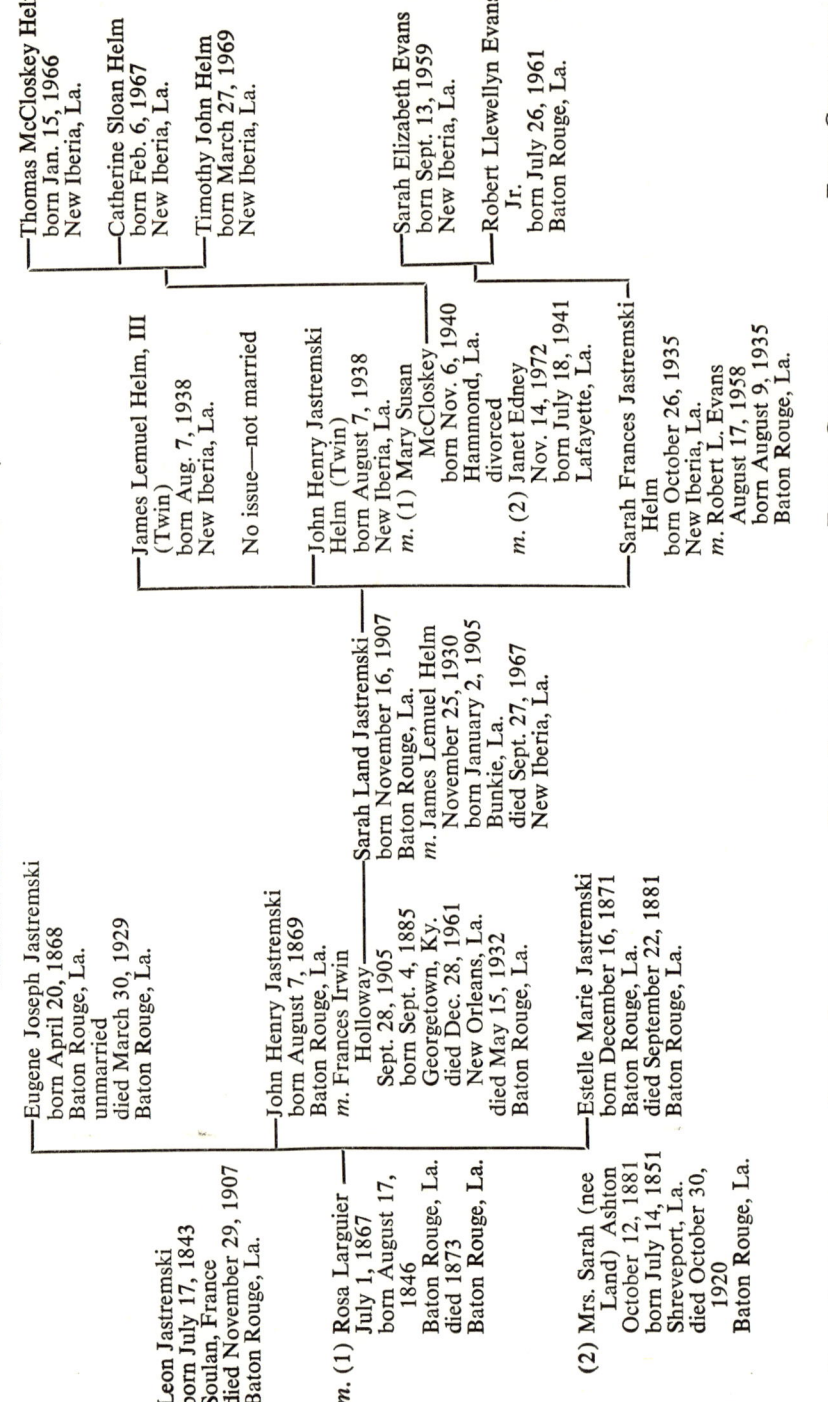

APPENDIX 2

SELECTED LETTERS

(Translated from French)

New Orleans, December 10, 1860

Dear Brother:

Since I left Baton Rouge, I have not heard from you and I admit it is my fault, my great fault, because as I did not write to you, you could not answer me. But I am going to give you my reasons, good or bad!

Some days after returning to the city, I read in a newspaper that they were looking for a journeyman printer in the office of "L'Amite Democrat" in Liberty, Mississippi, and that they were offering 35 dollars per month with board and room. You can imagine that I was not backward and as soon as I got a letter of introduction from the agent of the newspaper, I went to Liberty where I was accepted on my arrival. I arrived in the evening and the following morning I began to work and I worked there for three weeks, during which time I learned to my extreme embarrassment that the office was insoluble and the expenses enormous and the income was not sufficient to keep two workers at 35 dollars and their board and room at 45. Consequently, afraid of getting more deeply enmeshed in this hornet's nest, I hurried to get away from there and to return here, not wanting to work for his Majesty the King of Prussia. Since that time (it is a month since then), I have done everything to find work in the printing shops and pharmacies but without success. Keays is returning to the city and he is preparing to go to Baton Rouge on Saturday to see about his things. From him I learned that Bradley at Abbeville had need of a clerk and consequently I wrote to him to ask what would be the highest wages that he could offer me and that if it suited me I would go there right away. I do not expect to receive an answer from him before the end of next week. It is hard to find a position here at this moment because instead of looking for employees, they are being discharged on all sides, which does not improve the situation of young people who are seeking employment.

I ask you to be kind enough to go to the office of the "Comet" and ask the foreman of the office if he could employ me and at the same time do the same at the "Advocate" because at this time they should need workers. If you do not succeed in getting work for me in a pharmacy, try in a dry goods store if there is a possibility. Let me know the results of your efforts as soon as you can if you have the opportunity to get me a position as I am beginning to get bored here without work and I continue to spend money without cease. You must know many people in Baton Rouge and you know my capacity. You will render me a service by helping me in this matter.

Up to the present I have done nothing but talk about myself. It is now time to talk about you and your family also. In your reply give me news of Mrs. Keays, my sister and my grand niece and don't forget Olivier. You will try to excuse me to him for not having written. But as I did not want to write to anyone before finding work (not even to you), he will understand the reason for my silence. At any rate, tell him I will write tomorrow. Give my regards to all as well as to my honored brother, who I hope is in good health.

I am, your Majesty, the most humble and most obedient of your servants, and brother,   /s/ Leon Jastremski

Address your reply to:
    Care E. F. Mioton & Co.

(Translated from French)

My Dear Brother: Abbeville, May 20, 1861

I received a letter from you in the last mail which gave me news about you and your family. I see that with you republican enthusiasm has also developed. With regard to me, I almost have a desire to start already but I have given up the idea until the battles really start. Then I will abandon the mortar to take up the rifle and sabre. While waiting, after having tried to organize a company of volunteers for immediate service, we have organized a stationary company, principally to learn how to drill and handle arms. We have as instructor a Frenchman who served in the French army and who consequently knows army drill. With regard to me, as soon as the war begins, I will quit my work and go to enlist in some good company and I will have the advantage of knowing how to drill. There is no enthusiasm in Vermilion parish. They all have a strong fear of the war and they often say to me: "Well, when the North comes here, we will really have the war and when that happens it is going to be terrible." It will be very hard to make soldiers of people like that. They are not made of good material.

The Guignon family is getting along fine. Mrs. "Tocteuse" Bead has just brought an heir into the world, ugly enough to cause fear according to the opinion of the mother. Just imagine!

Pay my respects to all the family and tell them that I am always a very good boy and that I talk a lot about politics. We hear the sound of the drum morning and evening in Abbeville.

Pay my respects to Olivier and everyone in general.

                                   Your brother,
                                   /s/ Leon Jastremski

I am sending you an extract from *Meridional.*

P.S. We have 70 in our company.

(Translated from French)

Camp Squatley, (Virginia)
Near Williamsburg
Sept. 24, 1861

My Dear Brother:

With great pleasure yesterday evening I received your letter dated the 14th of this month in which you told me that you had not heard from me. I am surprised at that because after receiving your first letter almost a month ago, I sent you an answer immediately. I think you will receive it before this one and that it will give you complete details of my adventures since my departure from Camp Moore, La.

Considering the above, I will only give you the news since my arrival here. We are camped on a strip of land that runs into the James River (here it is almost four miles wide) about six miles from a large town named Williamsburg. Yorktown is fifteen miles from here. We have been in this camp for a month and a half and up to the present we have not seen a trace of the enemy. For two weeks now we have been setting up batteries and making entrenchments as we expect an attack from the fleet and the Lincoln troops from day to day as we are situated in a place which is very important and which guards the route to Richmond by land. We are helped in our work by about 100 Negroes. As for me, I do not work at that as I was raised to corporal two weeks ago which relieves me from the shovel but I am obliged to supervise the workers. At the time of writing this I have just finished my 24 hours of guard duty. My little rank gives me charge of placing the sentries and relieving them every two hours. Every day there are three corporals on guard and each of us takes care of one third of the sentries.

The cold has commenced to make itself felt. Within a week it will be freezing every night. Then it will be uncomfortable for us. Our uniforms are already worn and are of light material and I doubt that the Government will give new ones for a long time. In this miserable country one can buy nothing, neither food nor clothes. I still have 35 dollars left and the Government owes me almost 25. In spite of that, it is as if I had nothing in my pocket—I can obtain nothing. I am very grateful for your generous offer. I am going to tell you the things I need at present and which I will need more and more. These are a soldier's greatcoat, a pair of heavy gloves, two pairs of woolen socks, two pairs of flannel drawers, and also a military cap. If you can send these few articles, winter will pass more easily for me. From what they tell me, the snow is sometimes five feet deep. The James River and other rivers are covered with ice. You can imagine what that will be.

If you can get me these clothes send them as soon as possible by way of Adam's Express.

Pay my respects to all the family and embrace them for me.
Write soon!

Your Brother,
/s/ Leon Jastremski

(Translated from French)

Camp Marigny, near Yorktown.
October 22, 1861

Dear Brother:

I have just received your last letter which has given me a great deal of pleasure because it is very seldom that one receives news from Louisiana. I have not yet received the articles that you sent me but I hope they will not be long in arriving here because I am beginning to have real need for them. The weather is beginning to get cold. In a letter that Bradley wrote me from Abbeville I saw that Vermilion parish had sent me a winter suit and that he personally had sent me two blankets. So if I receive these things I will not be cold for the winter. Thank God!

Since my last letter we have changed camp and we have been approached by the Yankees. We are only separated from them by seven miles. The other day we tried to get them to leave their fortifications so that we could give them battle, but they did not want to take the bait. We waited for them a whole day. We had about three thousand men. Lying in high grass the height of a man we waited impatiently for them with our artillery, but in vain. Seeing that they would not come, we returned to camp. There was a skirmish here yesterday afternoon, but we do not know the details. We have orders to be prepared to march at any moment because a great battle is in preparation at this end. And I do not doubt that a serious engagement shall have taken place before you receive my letter. Twelve wagons loaded with scaling wagons passed here three days ago and it is probable that we are going to make an assault on the (walled) fortress. This is the opinion of many people. At any rate, something important is being prepared here. I have heard that an expedition of forty vessels with 30,000 men is now at the mouth of the York River. It is not known if this fleet is destined to disembark here in order to march on Richmond or if it will move to the south to attack some other place. In any case, if they come to us, they will have their work cut out for them, even though they are more numerous than we are. The 10th regiment is impatient for a fight. Yesterday evening, when the ranks were formed, we received orders to be ready at all times, and shouts of joy were heard all over the camp. The sick people and all are ready to march to meet them, even Capt. Dickey's Negro cook, who came to ask for a musket and ammunition and who asked the captain to let him go with us against the enemy. He was given permission as well as a gun and he is ready to enter our ranks to crush the Yankees.

You told me in your letter that you had not been able to find a cap for me but that if I needed one you would be able to send it to me. If you could send me one, it would be of great service to me. A black cap, or a blue one, or even a gray one. I am sending you my measure, which is that of the string I an enclosing in this letter. If you do this, you will oblige me.

Give my regards to all the family and embrace them—do not forget Olivier.

When the things that you are sending me arrive, I will write you another letter.

While awaiting your news, I thank you for all your kindness and remain,

Your brother,
/s/ Leon Jastremski

I have received two packages of newspapers from you up to now and it gives me a lot of pleasure when I receive them as there is not much amusement here.

Write me often.

(Translated from French)

Camp Marigny, Va., December 9, 1861

My dear Brother:

I have received two letters from you without being able to reply before this time for the reason that we have done nothing but go back and forth from Newport News, from Bethel and other places. That is the reason I have not written that I have received the box of clothes that you sent me. I have had it for more than a month and its contents serve me very well as it has already got very cold and we have already seen a little snow, but at the moment the weather is pleasant. I ask you to accept my sincere thanks for the generous present you have given me. Do not forget my sister, Leontine, either, for the trouble she took in preparing it. I will never forget this timely favor you have done me. I believe that now I will be all right for the winter. Now I will give some news about the state of the war at this end. Two weeks ago we returned from an expedition that we made to Great Bethel and beyond that and which lasted fifteen days, during which time we gathered some corn which was within the reach of the Yankees. We set out each morning from Bethel and returned in the evening to pass the night there, lying on our blankets around a fire. The day before our return to the camp, the news was given to General Magruder that the enemy was crossing at a place which was called "New Market Bridge", 10,000 men strong and with artillery. We were given orders to take up positions behind the same batteries at Bethel that had already given such a terrible lesson to the Yankees. We waited impatiently for them a whole night, thinking that at any moment fire would open up but morning arrived and still no enemy. The company of Donaldsonville gunners was at our side and thought that if they should ever fight they would not shame the Washington Artillery, although their horses are not well trained for the guns. I have seen the battle-field of Bethel and the place where the cannon-balls struck. There is a house which was pierced several times. I have visited the place where Colonel Winthrop of New York was killed and I am sending you a piece of the trunk of the tree where he had climbed to urge on his men to battle.

Today we were ordered to send our sick troops and heavy baggage to Williamsburg, which is located fifteen miles from here, because news has reached General Magruder that the enemy is disembarking a large number of men at Newport News. The order was given for not a single man to leave the camp as we are going to march within two days or perhaps within two hours as an enemy attack is expected. They are preparing to go to Richmond to drink their Christmas eggnog in that place. I believe a battle is imminent and that soon the 10th Louisiana Regiment will meet with them and an omelet will be made. As for me, I am impatient to fight in order to be able to boast (if my time is not up) of having seen battle. I have a position in the regiment where I can distinguish myself. I am one of the eight corporals who guard the flag and I march behind the flag carrier. When the battle line is formed it is placed behind me. If it is hit by a bullet, I assure you, I will have my hand on the flag before anyone else.

Dear Brother, I will finish this letter now, thanking you for what you sent me and with my regards to all the family. Embrace everyone for me and write soon.

I will write you again in a few days if there is news. In the meantime, I remain,

Your devoted brother
/s/ Leon Jastremski

Send me some newspapers as I get bored. We have built our winter quarters and the nights are long.

(Translated from French)

Camp Marigny, Virginia, March 23, 1862

Capt. J. Jastremski,

My Dear Brother:

It was with great pleasure that I received your letter of the 10th of this month. As I did not receive another letter from you I only could think of that. But the mail is so uncertain at present that everyone suffers from it for the reason that one can hardly send a letter to its destination. I have nothing new to tell you. I am still a Sergeant Major and as I am pretty popular in the regiment, it is possible that before long I will advance to a higher position.

This morning two men from one of our companies came to ask me to accept the position the third lieutenant in their company. They assured me that the majority of their company would vote for me. The election will take place in a week or two and it is possible that I will succeed in getting this rank. While waiting I am satisfied with the rank I hold at present, but if I can get advancement, you understand, I will not have any objection. I saw with pleasure that you are a militia captain. Consequently, if you are obliged to enter the campaign, at least you will earn good pay. That is always worth something more than the title. In your letter you tell me that you are sending me clothes. I am very pleased with that as it will help me a lot. At the same time I ask you to accept my sincere thanks for your kindness to me. And if I can ever help you in any way, you may be sure your brother will not show himself to be ungrateful. I am no longer such a show-off as I used to be and I am beginning to see things clearly in this world. Every day I learn to judge faces and see what life is. If I have the chance to come out of this war safe and sound, I will be able to handle matters.

As regards the war on the peninsula, I have nothing new to tell you, other than that a secret and dangerous expedition is being prepared on our part. Three hundred volunteers have been taken from the regiments. Although I did not lack the desire to be among this number, the embarrassing position that I hold and which does not permit me to leave camp for even one day, is the only thing which prevented me from taking part. I think that in two or three weeks you will have the results of this expedition, which, if we are successful, will bring a lot of glory to the victors.

We have had plenty of false alarms these days. They caused us to go on marches that were both difficult and useless. The roads are terrible and the season is rainy. I spent the night before last in the open air with the rain on my back, wrapped up in my blanket without a fire as we had been forbidden to light one, as we were too close to the enemy. You can imagine how disagreeable it was, but it did not bother my health in any way. I have become used to all kinds of weather. When the good weather comes again, I believe we will receive a visit from the Yankees. We are already preparing to give them a warm reception. We will give them a good lunch and a "gumbo" of grape-shot as sauce *piquante*.

Give my regards and thanks to your wife and embrace my grand niece and all the family in general. I recently wrote to Henry Keays and I expect a reply from him.

I am, your devoted brother,
/s/ Leon Jastremski

Send me some newspapers from time to time.

(Translated from French)

Camp Marigny, Va., April 7, 1862

Dear Brother:

I will quickly give you some news.

We have been fighting here since the 5th of this month—three days following each other. The enemy has not yet mounted an assault, but they bombarded us all day the day before yesterday and all day yesterday and today they are placing batteries in front of us. Up to the present we have had only two killed and some wounded. Yesterday we blew up an ammunition wagon of theirs and the result of the explosion is not known. There are constant skirmishes and continuous rifle fire. I believe they are going to attack us strongly tomorrow or the day after tomorrow. We are receiving reinforcements every moment. We are being attacked on three fronts: Yorktown, Wind's Mills and here, Lee's Mill. Up to the present we have repelled them on all sides and we have the advantage. I feel sure of success, in our favor. I am well, untouched and not afraid of them.

Adieu,
/s/ Leon Jastremski

APPENDIX 3

Platform of General Jastremski for Governor in 1903

Enunciated at a mass meeting in the Court House of Shreveport, Sept. 8, 1903.

I had not intended to begin either a partial or general personal canvass of the State until later, but the unaccountable suppression of my name from the list of gubernatorial candidates, in some of the New Orleans papers, coupled with the ignoring of my advocacy of the primary, has led me to come here and elsewhere at this time to give personal evidence that I am in the race and to the last ditch. I have not been terrified by the parade of the fifteen city bosses through the rotunda of the St. Charles Hotel to the Blanchard headquarters. I have never sought to bargain with these self-constituted masters of the people of New Orleans. On the contrary, I have exposed the abominable methods by which they have maintained their dictatorship and occupancy of the public offices in the commercial metropolis of the State for twenty or more years. I believed some months ago that the time had come for the people of the State to shake off the rule of these bosses who have lorded it too long in New Orleans and have extended their baneful influence into the country parishes.

In announcing my candidacy, therefore, in May last, I made the declaration that I would contend for nominations by primary for the State officers in this campaign, and that I would advocate the passage of a law by the next legislature requiring all nominations to be made by primary election. I also declared for the abridgement of the executive patronage. To the city bosses these propositions are as unacceptable as holy water is to Old Nick. By this abridgement I mean that the extraordinary powers conferred upon our governors to keep down Negro supremacy should not be continued over the white people.

Boss rule in New Orleans has practically estranged from the government thousands of the best manhood in that city, and particularly does it seem to have turned adrift hundreds of Confederate veterans who had fought for the State and the South and who, in not a few instances, had left limbs upon the battlefields. In consequence, many of these brave

Louisiana soldiers, unable to find employment, have had to seek refuge in the Soldiers Home. The places that they could have filled with fidelity and efficiency have been given to ward heelers.

I owe to the people of the State whatever distinction I may have gained, and I could not better manifest my gratitude for their goodness than by contending to the last for their liberation from a political system which is a reproach to a free country. I believe too that the men who seek gubernatorial honors should stand for something more than the gratification of their personal ambitions. They ought to stand above everything else for the right of the citizen and his liberties.

Nobody can assert that the principles that I have announced are undemocratic for they aim at placing the government where it belongs—with the people. To advocate "equal rights for all and special privileges to none" is a kind of Democracy that bossism and its allies regard as high treason. Having done this, and being resolved to continue till the fight is won, I may expect to be assailed in every conceivable way and with the foulest devices known to ward politics. To spread reports of my withdrawal from the contest has already been resorted to and I expect to see them renewed periodically during the campaign.

Driven to the primary election, the city bosses know that they cannot throw the whole strength of New Orleans to name a candidate as they have so often done in the conventions. How many votes will be cast for the opponents of their candidate they cannot estimate, so that the division of the votes in New Orleans will, they fear, leave their candidate at the short end. Realizing these difficulties the bosses will make the fight of their lives. Defeat means the dispersion of their system to the four winds. They are well organized and the people are not. Hence, the people should proceed to organize Equal Rights Clubs in every locality. With these clubs they will be enabled to insure a fair conduct of the primary, get their forces in hand, and shake off political methods that it is high time to suppress.

The rules of the Democratic Parish committee, under which the bosses maintain their domination over New Orleans, are simply monstrous and I have wondered how that brave population, which sent forth the heroic White Leaguers on the 14th of September, 1874, have so long submitted to them. To be a candidate against the boss of the ward it is requisite to organize a faction of not less than 250 qualified Democratic voters. No primary to vote directly for candidates other than delegates is permitted, and each faction must vote with its own distinct tickets. No ticket is counted which is in violation of this rule. This is tantamount to voting with open tickets, so that the boss can tell exactly how the voting is proceeding and also blacklist those who have the temerity to vote against him.

Except in times of public upheaval when the majority of the white people revolt, as in 1888 and 1896, and whip the bosses, horse, foot and dragoons, out of the offices, but not from the control of the party organizations, the bosses usually get the delegates to the parish and city conventions and as these delegates do their bidding, the bosses practically name all the city officials; and, by combinations, they have come well night naming the State officials for the past twenty-five years.

Four years ago the bosses concluded to take full charge of the State and they brought forward for governor Chief Boss John Fitzpatrick. No less a personage than Senator McEnery had been chosen to put him in nomination before the convention. Now the bosses are supporting Judge Blanchard and Senator McEnery is to figure as chairman of his campaign committee. It is easy to see, therefore, the drift of things, and that Judge Blanchard's election would give us four years more of boss influence and a return to the convention system, without which bossism will reach the end of its tether in this State.

The fight, therefore, is plainly marked. It stands with Judge Blanchard and his allies, the city bosses, who submitted to this coming primary only under duress, and who want no such thing as the abridgement of the executive patronage on one side. On the other stands the mass of the liberty loving white Democrats of this State, who won the primary fight and demand the abridgement of the patronage. It is with them that I want to march to victory and to the enthronement of real Democracy in Louisiana.

In entering this second phase of my campaign for the gubernatorial nomination, I desire to submit without ambiguity or reservation whatsoever, the views that will govern me in the event of my election.

There are two distinct systems of government. The first is the autocratic or monarchial system, and it is based on the theory that the masses are incapable of governing themselves. The other is the republican or democratic system, and it is based upon the opposite theory that "all men are created equal and are endowed by their Creator with certain inalienable rights; that among these are life, liberty and the pursuit of happiness. That to secure these rights, governments are instituted among men deriving their just powers from the consent of the governed." Any person with ordinary intelligence should be able easily to distinguish one system from the other, and to point out what measures or practices are autocratic and subversive of popular or democratic government.

Now that we have, admittedly, an intelligence and patriotic electorate, fully capable of governing wisely every locality in the State and the State in general, a further prolongation of the emergency powers that were conferred upon our governors since the reconstruction should be regarded as an unjustifiable subversion of the rights of our electorate. If the people of this State cannot now be trusted with the power of governing themselves, when will they be able to do it? We should be careful not to engraft in our body politic those powers that were recognized as provisional merely, authorizing the governor to appoint officials whom the people formerly elected. It is impossible for him to know every man who is recommended for appointment to office, and he must, necessarily, repose confidence in some people in every locality to certify to the character and fitness of the applicants. Not infrequently his confidence is placed in persons who are more interested in their own political fortunes than they are in the public good. When we consider the number of officers that the governor appoints under the existing laws, and the number of vacancies that he has to fill in the State, parochial and municipal offices, from the justices of the Supreme Court to the constable, we can imagine the magnitude of the burden that our Constitution and laws have imposed upon him, also the corresponding extent of the curtailment in the right of the people to elect their public servants. How much of the time that legislators should devote to their legitimate functions as law makers is spent in looking after the appointment of constituents and friends to some office? And, correspondingly, how much more time to look after the affairs of the State would not the governors have if he were relieved of this no longer necessary duty?

I remember when the various municipalities called their elections, appointed the commissioners, received the returns and declared the result. No commissions were issued by the governor, for these and other local officers, nor did he fill the vacancies therein by appointment as is done under the laws which have been obtained since the inception of reconstruction. This is but an illustration of a system of government which was born in dire necessities and with which every Democratic administration from that of Nicholls to the present one has been handicapped, and for the retention of which no good reason can be advanced. I desire to state most emphatically that my opposition to the continuation of this system, which was created and maintained by the Constitutions of 1868, 1879 and 1898, and the laws enacted thereunder, does not arise from its improper use by our Democratic governors, for I believe that all of them have sought to apply it for what they believed to be the best interests of the State. I object to it because it is contrary to the principles of "government by the people, of the people and for the people." No governor has operated this system of government more conscientiously and considerately than has Governor Heard. Nor have any of his predecessors administered the affairs of the State with more success. He has been untiring in his efforts for the promotion of the public welfare, and his administration will rank among the most beneficial in the annals of the State.

I favor public education to the fullest limits of the capabilities of the people and the State to sustain it, and I believe that the means to support and promote public education should be largely provided by local taxation, as the people then would take more interest and pride in their local schools. Logically, they should be given the right to elect the school boards by whom the school funds are to be applied and who are to supervise the conduct of the schools.

I also favor the election of the tax assessors by the people, for the plain reason that a far greater amount of taxes is required to support the parish and municipal governments, the schools, the levees, etc., than goes to the support of the State government from the limited six mills tax. The State, which has the least share of the taxes, has, under the present system, the selection of the assessing officer, when, under all the equities, the greater local interests, and the people who have all the taxes to pay should elect him. The people could not without injury to all their local interests elect assessors who would undervalue the taxable property. Besides, the police juries, elected by the people, are the reviewers of the tax rolls, hence the plea that the State's interest demands the appointment of this officer by the governor is not well grounded. If we turn back to the times when the assessors were elected by the people we shall find that the assessments were no less satisfactory than they have been under the appointive system. I therefore favor the passage of laws by the next General Assembly providing for the election of these local officials by the people, but in the meantime and in consonance with my conviction that through a well guarded primary election system, we shall attain the most perfect democratic government. I would appoint to these offices uniformly the nominees of a primary election. Furthermore, I would approve every law of the General Assembly changing statutory appointive offices into elective offices.

Believing that performances offer better guarantees than mere promises, I shall, preferably, point to my record to indicate what my attitude shall be toward certain matters of public interest.

Referring to education, I have to submit that from 1881 to 1888 I had the honor of serving as vice president of the Board of Supervisors of the Louisiana State University and Agricultural and Mechanical College, an honorary position not exempt from labor and responsibilities. I may also add that I have never permitted an opportunity to pass to befriend the cause of public education. I yield to none in my unbounded appreciation of the importance of the agricultural interests of the State, and during my incumbency of the office of State Commissioner of Agriculture and Immigration, to which I was called by Governor Foster, I was sparing no effort for its progress. I was, at the same time, afforded exceptional opportunities to acquaint myself with its needs and possibilities. I advocated them, as I have since, and shall continue to do in the future, unstinting State aid for general instruction in agriculture, for thorough experiments in improved methods of cultivation, in stock raising, and in irrigation, through which I firmly believe that our agricultural interests will attain a level of success that will surpass the most helpful estimates of the value, capabilities and productiveness of our soil.

My friendship for labor in all its branches, and my sincere desire for its welfare, has been practically demonstrated whenever I have been so fortunate as to occupy the relation of an employer.

My implicit faith in the policy of inviting immigration and belief in the benefits to be derived therefrom are so much of record as not to require any fresh assurances from me.

The maintenance of the levees and the protection of our lowlands from floods, also the improvement of the navigation of the Mississippi and the smaller streams in our State, have always received my zealous advocacy. In the Trans-Mississippi Congress, at Cripple Creek, I presented resolutions which were adopted, supporting these interests, and also secured endorsement for co-operation among the Trans-Mississippi states to divert the flood waters of numerous streams to irrigate the arid lands, and incidentally relieve the pressure upon our levees. I had previously advocated our levee interests before the National Board of Trade, the Western Waterways Conventions, the Industrial Conventions, the National Editorial Convention, and other bodies, which have influence upon legislation. I have been a constant advocate of manufactures of all kinds, of lumber, mining and other industries, the development of all the resources of the State, the construction of railroads, good roads, and all public improvements.

Regarding the foreign commerce of New Orleans and the country in general, I may be permitted to point to my labors while in the consular service which have received the highest official commendation, also to my persistent advocacy of the Isthmian canal, the Inter-oceanic railway and other means of enlarging our commerce. In summarizing, I may add that during the many years of my journalistic career, I have constantly supported these and other interests, the maintenance of law and order, and every measure calculated to promote the progress of the State and the welfare of its population.

It is almost superfluous for me to say that I hold in fraternal affection my comrades-in-arms of the Confederate army and their widows. The State can never be too generous to these men who, in their young manhood, responded so nobly to the call of its constituted authorities, to repair to the field and offer up their lives in defense of her sovereignty and rights. The State's obligations toward these heroic men, or their loved ones who are unprovided for, needs no elaboration; neither have

I need to announce my inflexible intention to urge the fullest possible observance of these most sacred obligations of the State. There is, besides, the attendant duty of inaugurating the compilation of the glorious history of our Louisiana troops in the great war and the recording of their names as precious heirlooms for their descendants.

I pledge myself, if elected, to ceaseless endeavors to carry out the views and policies above enunciated, and I also pledge myself to give force and application, as far as I may be able, to the true principles of Democracy and justice.

Appendix 4

General Jastremski's Position on Labor

Text of speech made at Washington Artillery Hall, Jan. 8, 1904

"Mr. President, Ladies, and Fellow-Democrats of New Orleans: Some few weeks ago with several of my friends I went to the city of Shreveport to address a meeting of the Democrats of that portion of the State, and while awaiting the hour of the meeting I received a telegram from New Orleans signed by the officers of the United Labor League to the effect that the League had unanimously given me their endorsement for governor and that they had likewise endorsed the platform which I have been advocating from the time of the announcement of my candidacy. During the meeting that night I had this welcome telegram read. This meeting represented all walks in life; the merchant, the farmer, the artisan and the laboring citizens of Shreveport, and of the neighboring country, and when that telegram was read, it elicited thunderous and continuous applause. That representative meeting of democrats were delighted to hear that the laboring men of New Orleans were ready to stand shoulder to shoulder in this coming fight for democratic principles and for the return to the people of home rule and the election of public officials from the town constable to the chief justice of the Supreme Court.

It was a glorious thing, this patriotic movement on the part of the United Labor League, and I will say that they were acting with their full strength for the restoration of the rights of the white citizens of the State.

It has been said that there was a dicker, a dicker with labor bosses, and that there was no difference between a dicker of that kind and a dicker with the political bosses of New Orleans. There is a great difference my fellow-citizens, and that is that the labor bosses, as they are called by some of the papers supporting Mr. Blanchard, and the laboring men for whom these bosses speak did not make a dicker for the purpose of office and public patronage, but they made this dicker, if you will call it so, for the purpose of restoring the true Democracy in the State of Louisiana. Whereas the bosses in their dickers have in view, not the restoration of the rights of the people to govern themselves, but simply to continue themselves in office and to continue to reap the benefits of public patronage. That is the difference between the two dickers. On the one side stands the great body of the people, the business men, the farmers and the laboring men, standing shoulder to shoulder, supporting this platform for the common rights of all, and on the other side stands my opponent endorsed by the bosses looking forward to a continuation of an autocratic, and not a democratic, form of government in the State of Louisiana, a continuance of one-man power which bestowed public patronage, not for the public benefit, but for the benefit of the politicians.

I am proud tonight to see this splendid audience. This meeting is a reiteration of the telegram that I received in Shreveport. It shows that that telegram was voicing the sentiments of the laboring men in New Orleans. And that it was irrevocable in its character; that the line of working men, farmers, merchants, businessmen, and of all classes of men in Louisiana cannot be broken on the 19th of January. As there are many speakers to follow me I shall make my remarks very brief. I want to say inasmuch as it has been stated in the papers that I would define my position toward the laboring men, that in common with every intelligent citizen I regard the laboring men as the bone and sinew of the country. It is from labor that all wealth springs and it is entitled to the greatest consideration of all men. At the same time the intelligent laborers know that they cannot use their strong arms, especially nowadays, without the assistance of capital and it ought to be the effort of every good citizen, of every public man, of every statesman to do all he possibly can to maintain the most friendly relations between these two great forces, labor and capital. These two forces are represented in our midst tonight, all aiming at the same results, the public good. I want to say to you, Mr. President and fellow-citizens, that if I am elected, as I expect to be, it shall be my aim to extend the greatest consideration to the laboring men, to give the same consideration to their requests or demands that can be claimed by any other class or force in the social and political body. They will have the same courteous reception in the executive office, the same consideration of their requests, the same courteous attention that the greatest capitalist in the State or in the world could expect to receive. They will be, as well as other classes of society, always welcome in the executive office. And it shall be my effort to promote such legislation as will harmonize as much as it can be done, and I hope thoroughly, all the differences that may arise between these two great forces of capital and labor. Marching together as we are doing in this campaign, I do trust, my fellow-citizens, that this political union of all these forces will subsist in the upbuilding of all the interests of the commonwealth and of the people, and of the interests of capital and labor as well.

I want to say a few words in regard to union labor. I always speak plain; I never try to ride two horses, nor try to. I want to say that I was reared in a printing office. At the age of fourteen, I had to get on a soap box in order to reach the type-setter's case to learn the art of all arts, and at that age already I knew of the existence of the Typographical Union, which was pointed out as the aid of every apprentice. Membership in the Typographical Union was the goal to which the apprentice aspired. When I became State printer in 1882, the printers in my office, before the pending session, came to me, they were my friends, and asked me to permit them to form a union, assuring me that it was to my interest. I consented to the formation of a branch of the Typographical Union, and the result was better and more reliable workmen. If you will go through any, or all of the great newspaper offices in the United States, you will find that they are operated by union labor, and that the disagreements which used to arise frequently, when the union was in its infancy, became fewer and fewer and now it is seldom that we have occasion to record a strike in a printing office. So then my friends when we come to consider that the labor unions in every branch of trade are conducted by more conservative men and that they have learnt more as to the best manner of conducting these unions, we can hope that what the Typographical Union has done in the way of harmonizing the employer and employee in the printing office will likewise be accomplished in all other branches of trade. It should be the aim of every good citizen to assist in removing the antagonism between these forces, for we must recollect that far back into the centuries there existed trade ills, and the trade unions, so that it is not a new thing in the history of our country, and I want to say to you, my fellow-citizens, that it shall be my aim as I have already said, when Governor of the State to do all that is possible to reconcile the differences between these forces.

I believe that my platform of principles is well known. I believe that it is known that I favor a compulsory primary election law in order that the people of New Orleans, this summer and fall, may, for the first time in decades of years, be enabled, under protection of the law, to nominate by primary election the next city government, from mayor down to the councilmen. And I shall recommend to the Legislature that that law be passed. I shall also recommend to the Legislature that they proceed with the adoption of laws curtailing, to the last degree, the executive patronage of the governor, in order that the people may enjoy their right to elect public officials, and enjoy the blessings of home rule and of popular government. I shall also recommend to the Legislature that all unnecessary offices, all the sinecures, be abolished, and that the government be economically administered in order that all the sums levied upon the people may be applied to legitimate and proper purposes, and then, my fellow-citizens, considering that the assessments of the State are continually increasing from year to year, in the last two years the increase in assessments having reached the enormous figures of thirty-five millions, that steps be taken whereby, as the assessments increase, the rate of taxation shall be reduced. I will not go on at further length, but I believe I have sufficiently outlined my position on this question. Thanking you from the bottom of my heart for the reception you have given me, I shall now yield the floor to the next speaker.

Appendix 5

Votes for Governor of Louisiana in Primary Election, Jan. 19, 1904.*

	GOVERNOR	
PARISHES	Blanchard	Jastremski
Orleans—Ward 1	1,226	354
Ward 2	1,348	338
Ward 3	1,632	754
Ward 4	781	201
Ward 5	1,391	145
Ward 6	927	272
Ward 7	1,133	748
Ward 8	703	241
Ward 9	824	462
Ward 10	1,522	683
Ward 11	1,120	803
Ward 12	657	482
Ward 13	870	215
Ward 14	567	354
Ward 15	769	232
Ward 16	310	106
Ward 17	310	163
Total for Orleans	16,090	6,553
Acadia	953	875
Ascension	415	311
Assumption	778	78
Avoyelles	524	680
Bienville	619	444
Bossier	212	287
Caddo	1,379	1,075
*Calcasieu	1,473	1,437
Caldwell	218	148
*Cameron	170	174
Catahoula	648	479
Claiborne	524	577
Concordia	168	70
De Soto	355	591
East Baton Rouge	473	823
*East Carroll	116	61
East Feliciana	261	233
Franklin	248	306
Grant	266	165
Iberia	586	721
Iberville	408	454

	GOVERNOR	
PARISHES	Blanchard	Jastremski
Jackson	436	179
Jefferson	1,090	64
Lafayette	459	996
Lafourche	1,046	460
Lincoln	238	184
Livingston	275	184
Madison	101	72
Morehouse	344	166
Natchitoches	548	554
Ouachita	531	500
Plaquemines	550	113
Pointe Coupee	271	399
Rapides	811	479
Red River	324	148
Richland	151	253
Sabine	403	535
St. Bernard	383	61
St. Charles	191	123
St. Helena	160	139
St. James	442	172
St. John	290	32
St. Landry	1,050	2,264
St. Martin	368	436
St. Mary	873	269
St. Tammany	491	216
Tangipahoa	507	370
Tensas	153	38
Terrebonne	308	892
Union	357	241
Vermilion	283	1,220
Vernon	467	293
Washington	144	98
Webster	260	437
West Baton Rouge	113	254
West Carroll	145	93
West Feliciana	236	200
Winn	430	260
Total for State	42,113	29,957

*One precinct did not make returns. †Two precincts did not make returns.
*Report of Secretary of State, January 1, 1905, pp IX-XI.

APPENDIX 6

Gen. Jastremski's Platform for Governor in 1907

BATON ROUGE, LA., February 25, 1907.

Fellow-Citizens and Democrats:

Agreeably with my conception of the spirit of the primary election system of nominating candidates, and with the deference that, as a candidate for the gubernatorial nomination, I feel is due you, I most respectfully submit for your consideration these, my views upon some of the principal questions of the hour. I shall deal with them as briefly as possible, and elaborate them later on.

Four years ago the Government of the State had no resemblance to the principles of Democracy. The election of the Governor carried with it the appointment by him, regardless of the people, of the local school boards and of *practically* the entire educational organization in the State; of the tax collectors in New Orleans, and the assessors throughout the State, in whose hands had virtually been vested the power to fix the assessment for State and local purposes of taxation. Never before, save under military rule, had this power, so violative of the principle of "no taxation without representation," been thus diverted. The Governor appointed innumerable other public officials and boards, and by appointment he also filled well nigh every vacancy arising in the offices, even in the few offices that the people were permitted to fill by election.

Party nominations were made by conventions that were governed chiefly by his appointees, and with the design of perpetuating the power and elevating to other offices men in affiliation with the powerful influences which he controlled.

Such was the political condition that, at the patriotic appeal of friends, who were afterwards joined by tens of thousands of the Democracy of Louisiana, I ventured to confront and to aid them to overthrow.

The widespread demand for nominations by primary election was met by providing rules and methods which permitted local primaries, which began months before the State primary of January 19, 1904, under various rules and qualifications wihch would not have qualified the participants in these local primaries to vote in the State primary nor in the general election. This was done, notwithstanding the system under which the successfully-conducted primary in Mississippi had been held, and which ought to have been followed in Louisiana.

A fair ascertainment of the sentiment of the Democracy of Louisiana was not to be expected under such conditions. As a loyal Democrat, I had accepted the rules formulated by the party organization, and as a loyal Democrat I acquiesced promptly in the announced results of the State primary.

But the principles of Democracy which were involved still lived and the question that arose after the primary was whether the contest for their rehabilitation was to be continued or abandoned. The consensus of opinion among my friends, and my own inclinaitons, were that it should be prosecuted, and my renewed candidacy is based upon this conclusion.

The prosecution of this contest has thus far resulted in the enactment of laws and constitutional amendments which have abolished the autocratic powers of the Governor and restored to the people the right to nominate their candidates by the direct, secret, Australian ballot. A primary election law, which, though it offers provisions which could and should be amended later, has been enacted, and will, if fairly conducted, meet the necessities of the case.

For this, however, the manhood of Louisiana must insist that the secrecy of the ballot shall no longer be subverted as it has been. There can be no justification for resorting to dark-lantern methods in our campaigns. We must get the free ballot and the fair count, if we would educate our youth in the lofty principles of true Democracy by which the people of Louisiana should be governed.

If we would keep pace with the march toward better days and better conditions, all good citizens should lend their influence to re-establish the sway of "equal rights for all and special privilege for none"; to resurrect the doctrines of "taxation limited to the necessities of government economically administered;" to a faithful observance and impartial execution of the laws; to the carrying out, in letter and spirit, the measures and principles which have been incorporated in the laws and the Constitution; and to the enactment of other laws which may be required for their attainment.

No retreat, no evasions, no temporizing in this should be tolerated.

The equalization of taxation is a question of the first importance, and Article 225 of the Constitution lays down these plain lines to attain it, viz.:

"Taxation shall be equal and uniform throughout the territorial limits of the authority levying the tax (the General Assembly, Police Juries, City or Town Councils, etc.), and all property shall be taxed in proportion to its value, to be ascertained as directed by law; provided, the assessment of all property shall never exceed the actual cash value thereof."

To conform with these and the other provisions in said article, I believe that all property should, as the basis for the assessment, be appraised at its fair actual cash valuation; then, that the assessment, for the purposes of State taxation, and to operate uniformly throughout the State, should be fixed by the General Assembly, at some rate or per cent. of the appraisement well below the appraisement. This would preclude assessments from exceeding the actual cash valuation or appraisement. This will inevitably arise in all cases of sudden declines in values. By this means, extreme fluctuations in the revenues would be avoided, since the gains and losses in values corresponding with the fractional assessment would be but fractional. It would be easy for the General Assembly to fix the per cent. of the State assessment upon the aggregate of the appraisement of all the taxable property in the State. The rate of the State tax could thereupon be more accurately and more equitably fixed.

In the same manner the local bodies should be required to fix the per cent. of the local assessment in accordance with the necessities of the locality over which their authority extends.

We would then cease to see the nominal cash valuation, which the law has vainly sought to convert into the assessment, oscillate, as it has done confessedly, between localities and individuals at anywhere from thirty-three and one-third to one hundred per cent.

Every taxpayer has the right to be informed of the amount of the appraisement of his property and of the per cent. of the State and the local assessments, respectively, based upon the appraisement. With such information appearing in his tax bills, he could calculate if any error or injustice has been done him, and seek such relief as he would be justified in demanding.

By these means, the taxing powers, State and local, would not come in conflict, as they have by the increases of State assessments, whereby special taxes particularly, and local taxes, too, were suddenly raised, largely in excess of the demands of the public obligations and of the local budgets. Taxation would be adjustable by the State and local powers for their needs, respectively, by reducing or raising the rate of taxation or the per cent. of the assessment.

The fare of three cents per mile for railway travel should be reduced to two cents, and the powers of the Railroad Commission enlarged to secure for the people the same protection in their rights and interests which are enjoyed in other States.

Louisiana is essentially an agricultural State; and, to enable the farmers and planters to transport their products to market and facilitate intercourse generally, the construction and maintenance of good roads is a matter of primal necessity. It demands earnest consideration and effective action from the State and the local governments. To assist in raising the means required for this object, all unnecessary offices should be promptly abolished, and all excessive fees, commissions and salaries now allowed to public officials should be revised and reduced to a basis just and equitable to those officials and to the taxpayers.

Immigration should be encouraged.

Adequate provision should be made for the levees, for public education, for the public and charitable institutions, and to meet all the public obligations.

I believe, too, that a sinking fund, however small it might at first seem, should be created to provide for a gradual reduction and payment of the public debt, and that steps should be inaugurated looking to the refunding of the bonded debt at a lower rate of interest.

Article 227 of the Constitution directs that, with other purposes, the taxing power shall be exercised to provide pensions for the Confederate soldiers and sailors, and their widows; to establish markers or monuments upon the battlefields of the country commemorative of the services of Louisiana soldiers on such fields; and to maintain a memorial hall in New Orleans for the collection and preservation of relics and memorials of the late Civil War.

These are sacred obligations, for which the most liberal provision should hereafter be made. A proper observance of all of these obligations will conduce to the upbuilding of the public pride, the patriotism and character of the people—considerations which it is the solemn duty of the Government of the State to constantly nurture and promote.

Publicity should be given to all transactions and acts of a public character, and every department of the Government should be strictly held within the limitations of its functions, as they are defined in the Constitution.

To all of the foregoing I pledge my faithful observance and efforts, if elected to the exalted office for which I most respectfully solicit your generous support.

With assurances of my unbounded consideration and of my most grateful appreciation of the very generous support with which you honored me in my first candidacy, I remain,

    Your most obedient servant,
            /s/ Leon Jastremski

BIBLIOGRAPHICAL NOTES

Chapter 1—Seeds of Glory

1. *Daily Advocate* clipping, undated, in Jastremski family papers, Helm Collection.
2. Henry Archacki, Capt. Leon Jastrzemski—Louisiana's Greatest Pole, *Straz,* May 21, 1970.
3. Sigmund H. Uminski, Two Polish Confederates, *Polish American Studies,* July-December, 1966, Vol. XXIII, No. 2, pp. 75-81; The Poles in the Civil War, *American Polonia Reporter,* Spring, 1965, p. 14.
4. Wilson to Kowalewski, Sept. 25, 1958, Archives of Captain Stanislaus Mlotkowski Memorial Brigade Society, hereinafter cited as Archives.
5. Kowalewski to Wilson, Oct. 1, 1958, Archives.
6. Conversation with Mrs. Charles Kilczewski, April 14, 1974.
7. Kowalewski to Wilson, Feb. 7, 1959, Archives.
8. Conversation with Charles Kilczewski, August 24, 1974.
9. Conversation with Mrs. Charles Kilczewski, Oct. 14, 1974; Vincent J. Kowalewski to War Dept., August 14, 1961, Archives.
10. Conversation with Charles Kilczewski, March 25, 1974.
11. Ernest Gueymard, Gen. Jastremski to Be Cited, *State-Times,* May 28, 1974.
12. Henry Archacki, Return to Fort Delaware, *Straz,* June 20, 1974.

    Edward Pinkowski, Captain Leon Jastremski—Prisoner in Fort Delaware, *Straz,* June 20 and July 4, 1974.

Chapter 2—Uprooted Lives

1. Wilbur L. Cross, *The History of Henry Fielding* (New Haven, 1918), Vol. 1, p. 1.
2. Kasper Niesiecki, *Herbarz Polski,* Vol. 4, pp. 470-471, translated by Henry Archacki, June 28, 1974. The name of Jastrzebski has a hook under the *e.* If the hook is not used, the name is spelled Jastrzembski to convey the sound of a hooked *e.* People with this name have always had to contend with certain annoyances because of the difficulties of spelling the name.
3. Tadeusz Sulimirski, *The Sarmatians* (New York, 1970), pp. 185-194.
4. ibid, p. 164.
5. ibid, p. 167.
6. In 1808, Napoleon issued an Imperial Decree creating the University of France, thereby taking autonomy away from all universities in France like the University of Montpellier. Afterwards, until the decree was rescinded in 1896, the universities issued diplomas in the name of French government. Research of Miss Moreen Kattie, Free Library of Philadelphia, April 25, 1974.

7. It is now located in Ukrainian Soviet Socialist Republic. Nowo Uschitzk is spelled on Ukrainian maps Nova Ushytaya, and Kamienietz Podolski is Kayanets' Podil's'ky. William Karpa, *The Map of Ukraine,* 1955, published by the League of Americans of Ukrainian Descent, Inc., Chicago.
8. Jerzy Piorkowski, "A Man Who Lived Too Long," *Poland,* October, 1974, pp. 30-32.
9. Medical diploma and medal citation in Jastremski family papers, Helm Collection.
10. Mrs. Sallie Land Jastremski Scrapbook, Helm Collection.
11. Castres to Jastremski, October 20, 1868. Helm Collection.
12. Bolek's *Who's Who in Polish America,* in a biography of Leon Jastremski, said he "came to America with his father, settling at first in Montreal, Canada, then came to Abbeville, La." The error was originally made, perhaps, in *Monitor Clevelandzki* (Cleveland Polish Monitor), Nov. 27, 1923, in a feature article, "Syn Powstanca Polskiego Bohaterem Walk o Wolnosc." For history of Vermilionville, see J. Philip Dismukes, *The Center: A History of the Development of Lafayette, Louisiana* (Lafayette, 1972); James W. Mobley, "The Academy Movement in Louisiana," *Louisiana Historical Quarterly,* July, 1947, Vol. 30, pp. 836-837; Donald J. Millet, "Town Development in Southwest Louisiana, 1865-1900," *Louisiana History,* Spring, 1972, Vol. XIII, pp. 139, 151-154; Harry Lewis Griffin, *The Attakapas Country—A History of Lafayette Parish,* Louisiana (New Orleans, 1959), which does not list Dr. Jastremski as the second doctor of Lafayette Parish.
13. See Documents No. 1074 and No. 2168, Clerk of Courts, Lafayette, La.
14. Document No. 1111, Clerk of Courts, Lafayette.
15. Document No. 1444, Clerk of Courts, Lafayette.
16. Document No. 1664, Clerk of Courts, Lafayette.
17. Document No. 2150, Clerk of Courts, Lafayette.
18. Cherry Hill Books, 202 Highland Ave., Cheshire, Conn., 1968.
19. Dr. Kowalewski (Cowelaski) left Liverpool, England, on the ship Orozimbo, Daniel Marcy, master, and arrived in New Orleans, Feb. 10, 1840, Passenger Lists, Book III, Port of New Orleans, p. 70, Howard-Tilton Library, New Orleans; Mrs. Marie Kowalewski (Koveleski) left Liverpool on the ship Virginia, Stephen Kenny, Master, and arrived in New Orleans, Jan. 15, 1841, ibid., p. 118.
20. For the family relationship, see Mobile *Register,* August 21, 1897; New Orleans *Times,* August 29, 1864.
21. Joyce Amedee to Pinkowski, Feb. 13, 1970; Joseph Nicholas Gorlinski, son of Thomas and Anne (nee Kwiatkowski) Gorlinski, married Valentine Cecile Wrotnowski, daughter of Stanislaus Auguste and Catherine (nee Cybulska) Wrotnowski, Jan. 1, 1851, with Rev. H. C. Gache, S. J., performing the ceremony in St. Joseph's Catholic Church, Baton Rouge. Three of their children were baptized in the same church on Dec. 31, 1859: Andrew Francis William, born Dec. 27, 1855, Elina (Helena) Cecile, born August 31, 1852, and Frank Adolphe Lafayette, born July 18, 1859. 1860 census, p. 83, revealed Joseph Gorlinski was

35 years old, Valentine, 27. For death of an infant child, Marie Josephine, on Nov. 15, 1863, see New Orleans *Times,* Nov. 17, 1863. For a bit of his career as an abolitionist and mapmaker, see New Orleans *Times,* Dec. 16, 1863; *Daily True Delta,* July 30, 1864; *The Era,* July 30, 1864.

22. From 1851 to 1865 Gorlinski owned a property within the city limits on the road leading from Baton Rouge to General Bernard's plantation. See New Orleans *Times* and *Bee,* March 9, 24 and April 10, 1865; Conveyance Records T, pp. 461-462 and P, p. 336, East Baton Rouge Parish, Baton Rouge. New Orleans Directory, 1857, with a section on Baton Rouge, listed Gorlinski's address on Third St., near Church St., and Mrs. J. Gorlinski was a music teacher in Mrs. M. W. Read's Academy on Church St., near Hypolite St.
23. New Orleans City Directory, 1857.
24. Baton Rouge, 12th census, 1860, p. 62, lists name as Fred Budinsky, 37, born in Prussia, his wife, Bridget, 24, born in Ireland, and four children, Liza, 7, Amelia, 6, Josephine, 2, and William A., 7 months, all born in Louisiana.
25. Baton Rouge, 1860 census, lists Corwin, 56, his wife, Eliza, 43, born in France, and four children, Elizabeth, 18, and Sophia, 13, born in France, John, 8, and Adelaide, 1, born in Louisiana.
26. Baton Rouge, 11th census, lists name as Lawry, 55, his wife, Sophia, 40, and Rosa, 17, all born in Poland.
27. August Pilitowski left Bremen on the barque Theodore Korner and arrived in New Orleans, July 5, 1841, Passenger Lists, Vol. III, p. 130.
28. Edward Bieganski died in New Orleans, Jan. 27, 1886, at the age of 75. New Orleans *Picayune,* Jan. 28, 1886.
29. Cohen's New Orleans and Lafayette Directory, 1850.
30. Documents No. 2168, No. 2169, No. 2397, No. 2398, No. 1963, No. 2077, and No. 2076, Clerk of Courts, Lafayette.
31. New Orleans *Times Democrat,* Nov. 3, 1893.
32. Rev. Msgr. Richard von Phul Mouton to Pinkowski, June 4, 1974.
33. Documents No. 2397, No. 2398, and No. 2614, Clerk of Courts, Lafayette.
34. SJP 5, p. 90, Catholic Life Center, Baton Rouge.
35. For a biography of Gueydan, see Alcee Fortier, *Louisiana,* Vol. 1, pp. 526-528; for residence in Abbeville, see 1860 census.
36. The lawsuit was referred to when bond of Mrs. Eugene I. Guegnon was returned and recorded Nov. 13, 1885, Conveyance Record No. 1, p. 788, Vermilion Parish, Abbeville.
37. Griffin, p. 117, said Guegnon was challenged to several pistol duels and was wounded in two of them. He died in Abbeville in 1862 at the age of 47.
38. William Henry Perrin, *Southwest Louisiana—Historical and Biographical* (New Orleans, 1891), stated E. I. Addison, born in Opelousas, La., Dec. 30, 1837, learned the trade of printer at Abbeville in "the office of the Meridional, then owned and edited by E. I. Guegnon, of which he had charge until the breaking out of the war."

39. Stanwood Jastremski, who died May 30, 1968, in Houma, La., was the last male descendant of the family to carry the Jastremski name. He was the youngest son of Dr. Leon H. Jastremski (1864-1931).

Chapter 3—The Big Soldier

1. *Capt. Leon Jastremski—Louisiana's Greatest Pole,* by Henry Archacki, *Straz,* May 21, 1970.
2. *The Daily State,* Baton Rouge, La., Nov. 29, 1907.
3. *Captain Leon Jastremski,* by Sigmund H. Uminski, Mlotkowski Memorial Room, Fort Delaware, 1970.
4. *The Poles in the Civil War,* Part xvi, by Sigmund H. Uminski, *American Polonia Reporter,* Spring, 1965, p. 14.
5. Tribute of Judge T. J. Kernan, *The Daily Picayune,* New Orleans, La., November, 29, 1907.
6. "Baton Rouge," by Col. James R. Randall, New Orleans, n. d.
7. Interview with Mrs. Sarah Jastremski Helm, New Iberia, La., April 24, 1974.
8. Leon Jastremski to John Jastremski, May 20, 1861, translated from French. Helm Collection.
9. ibid.
10. ibid.
11. ibid.
12. Leon Jastremski to John Jastremski, Dec. 10, 1860, translated from French by Patrick Darcy. Helm Collection.
13. Leon Jastremski to John Jastremski, Oct. 22, 1861, translated from French. Helm Collection.
14. Leon Jastremski's Military Service Record, National Archives, Washington, D. C.
15. *Truth* (Souvenir Edition), Confederate Re-Union, Baton Rouge, La., July 3-4, 1899.
16. Biographical sketch of Leon Jastremski, *Logansport Inter-State Journal,* c. 1903.
17. Leon Jastremski to John Jastremski, March 4, 1862, translated from French. Helm Collection.
18. *The Louisiana Tiger—Sulakowski,* by Col. Francis C. Kajencki, *Polish American Studies,* July-December, 1966, p. 84.
19. *Official Records of the Union and Confederate Armies,* Series 2, vol. XI, Part 1, p. 318.
20. Leon Jastremski to John Jastremski, Sept. 24, 1861, translated from French. Helm Collection.
21. *Charge of the Tenth Louisiana at Malvern Hill, Truth.*
22. General Clement A. Evans, *Confederate Military History,* Vol. 10, p. 34 (Atlanta, 1899).
23. *Charge of the Tenth Louisiana at Malvern Hill.*

24. ibid.
25. Journal of Lt. Col. Henry D. Monier, *Military Record of Louisiana*, p. 31.
26. ibid.
27. ibid.
28. Henry Thomas and Dana Lee Thomas, *50 Great Americans—Their Inspiring Lives and Achievements.* (New York, 1948).
29. Jastremski Military Service Record.
30. Monier's Journal, pp. 44-45.
31. Jastremski Military Service Record.
32. James Ford Rhodes, *History of the Civil War, 1861-1865.* (New York, 1961).
33. ibid, p. 219.
34. Frank Moore, editor, *Rebellion Record*, Vol. 7, p. 323. (New York, 1864).
35. *Confederate Military History*, Vol. 10, p. 254.
36. *Rebillion Record*, Vol. VIII, Part 2, p. 122.
37. Monier's Journal, p. 46.
38. *This is Gettysburg, Pennsylvania*, p. 6. (Gettysburg, 1969).
39. Bruce Catton, The Epic Story of Gettysburg, *The Reader's Digest*, July, 1957, p. 55.
40. Jastremski Military Service Record.
41. Bruce Catton, *The Army of the Potomac: A Stillness at Appomattox*, p. 39. (New York, 1953).
42. Don Congdon, editor, *Combat: The Civil War*, p. 471. (New York, 1967).
43. Roy P. Basler, editor, *The Collected Works of Abraham Lincoln*, Vol. VII, p. 324. (New Brunswick, N. J., 1953).
44. W. E. Woodward, *Meet General Grant*, p. 320. (Garden City, N. Y., 1928).
45. Bruce Catton, *Grant Takes Command*, p. 223. (Boston, Mass., 1968).
46. Adjutant General's Report, State of Louisiana, p. 22. (New Orleans, 1890).

Chapter 4—Prisoner of War

1. W. Emerson Wilson, *Fort Delaware.* (Newark, Del., 1957).
2. James St. C. Morton, *Memoirs of the Life and Services of Capt. and Brevet Major John Sanders of the Corps of Engineers, U. S. Army.* (Pittsburgh, Pa., 1861).
3. Stanislaus Mlotkowski Military Service Record, National Archives, Washington, D. C.
4. Samuel P. Bates, *History of Pennsylvania Volunteers, 1861-1865.* (Harrisburg, 1869-1871.
5. *The War of the Rebellion: A Compilation of the Official Records of the Union and Confederate Armies*, Series 2, Vol. 4, p. 23, cited hereinafter as *Official Records.*

6. ibid., Ser. 2, Vol. 8, pp. 986-1004.
7. *Truth.*
8. Diary of Lt. Joseph W. Mauck, 10th Virginia Infantry, mss., Confederate Museum, Richmond, Va.
9. Rev. Isaac W. K. Handy, *United States Bonds; or, Duress by Federal Authority,* n. p., 1874.
10. Helm Collection.
11. *Official Records,* Series 2, Vol. 6, pp. 890-891; Nancy Travis Keen, *Confederate Prisoners of War of Fort Delaware,* pp. 18-19, reprinted from *Delaware History,* Vol. XIII, No. 1, April, 1968.
12. Capt. George Baylor, 12th Virginia Cavalry, *Bull Run to Bull Run,* (Richmond, Va., 1900). Captain Baylor mentions that Captain Mlotkowski gave him a "nice silk tobacco purse," knitted by his wife, and tobacco, and also gave the Confederate prisoners five blankets.
13. Handy, *United States Bonds.*
14. Helm Collection. Captain Jastremski used the term, "sister," when he really meant sister-in-law, and the two persons he referred to by their first names were Henry and Oliver Keays.
15. ibid.
16. Diary of Thomas Pinckney of South Carolina, mss., Confederate Museum, Richmond, Va.
17. Sergeant Charles W. Rivenbark, 1st North Carolina State Troops, *Two Years at Fort Delaware,* Histories of the Several Regiments and Battalions from North Carolina (Goldsboro, N. C., 1901), IV. He wrote, "Every bone, horn, brass tack, bit of tin, wire or copper were appropriated to some purpose. Bushels of rings, pins, buttons, chains, charms and puzzles were patiently wrought out of such crude material."
18. Handy.
19. ibid.
20. Pinckney Diary.
21. Handy.
22. Major John Ogden Murray, *The Immortal Six Hundred.* (Winchester, Va., 1905) pp. 61-62.
23. Edward R. Rich, *Comrades Four* (New York, 1907) pp. 156-157, and Diary of Captain C. Dickinson, pp. 127-128.
24. Murray.
25. Helm Collection.
26. Handy.

Chapter 5—Ordeal of Fire and Starvation

1. The names of the officers who were exchanged by General Foster in July, 1864, appear in *Official Records,* Ser. 1, Vol. xxxvi, Pt. 2, p. 199 and pp. 147-148. The names of the 600 Confederate officers who were removed from Fort Delaware in August, 1864, appear in Handy, *United States Bonds,* pp. 632-645. In *Prison Life During the Rebellion,* by Fritz Fuzzlebug (Captain John J. Dunkle) (Singer's Glen, Va., 1869), p. 19, it is indicated that General Schoepf selected disabled officers, at least 100 of whom were useless to the Southern cause, if exchanged, because of their wounds, loss of arms or legs.
2. Proceedings of a General Court Martial, U. S. steamship *Delaware,* in the charges against Captain Daniel D. Latham and Second Mate William Baxter, Port Royal Harbor, S. C., August 25, 1864. War Records Division, National Archives. Hereinafter cited as Crescent Proceedings.
3. Diary of Captain Henry C. Dickinson, 2nd Virginia Cavalry, p. 63. Privately printed and limited to 225 copies. The copy I used was in the Rare Book Room, Library of Congress.
4. ibid.
5. Crescent Proceedings.
6. Log of U. S. Str. Admiral, War Records Division, National Archives.
7. Diary of Capt. Thomas Pinckney, p. 30, typewritten copy, Confederate Museum, Richmond, Va.
8. Dickinson Diary, p. 71.
9. Foster to Rear Admiral J. A. Dahlgren, August 30, 1864, *Official Records,* Vol. xxxv, Pt. 2, pp. 261-262.
10. Fuzzlebug, *Prison Life,* p. 24.
11. Diary of Lieut. S. T. Anderson, 1st S. C. Cavalry, p. 15. Confederate Museum, Richmond, Va.
12. Fuzzlebug, *Prison Life,* p. 25.
13. Luis F. Emilio, *History of the Fifty Fourth Regiment of Massachusetts Volunteer Infantry, 1863-1865* (Boston, 1894).
14. Dickinson Diary, p. 73.
15. Helm Collection.
16. For the use of the two batteries in the hands of the Confederates, see Life at Fort Wagner, by Capt. S. A. Ashe, *Confederate Veteran,* Vol. xxxv (1927), pp. 254-255; Perilous Adventure at Battery Wagner, by Judge H. D. D. Twiggs, *Confederate Veteran,* Vol. XII (1905), pp. 104-105; After the Evacuation of Battery Wagner, by Capt. S. A. Ashe, *Confederate Veteran,* Vol. 35 (1927), p. 451, and Life at Fort Wagner, ibid, p. 254.
17. Dickinson Diary, p. 77. He also stated that on October 6 the Federal forces opened up with a mortar gun from Fort Gaines and on the 7th with two guns from Fort Gregg.
18. Foster to Saxton, Sept. 12, 1864, *Official Records,* Ser. 1, Part II, Vol. XLVII, pp. 284-285.

19. Dickinson Diary, p. 77. For the experiences of other prisoners, see *Imprisoned under Fire*, the stories of Captain F. C. Barnes, 56th Virginia Infantry, and Captain R. E. Frayser, Signal Corps, in *Southern Historical Society Papers*, Vol. XXIV, pp. 365-377, reprinted from the Richmond, Va., *Times*, August 22, 1897; the story of Colonel Abram Fulkerson, 63rd Tennessee Infantry, *S. H. S. Papers*, Vol. XXII, pp. 127-146.
20. Saxton to Foster, Sept. 8, 1864. *Official Records*, Ser. 1, Vol. XLVII, Part II, p. 276.
21. Fuzzlebug, *Prison Life*, p. 29.
22. Dickinson Diary, p. 94, and Pinckney Diary, p. 39.
23. Notes on Dr. Louis Radzinski, by Joseph A. Borkowski, Pittsburgh, Pa.
24. Louis D. Radzinski Military Service Record, War Records Division, National Archives, and Emilio, *History of 54th Massachusetts Infantry*.
25. Fuzzlebug, *Prison Life*, p. 53.
26. Dickinson Diary, p. 96. Captain Dickinson described one of the attempts on Oct. 22 in some detail.
27. ibid, p. 160.
28. ibid, p. 98.
29. ibid, p. 99.
30. Murray, *The Immortal 600*, p. 130.
31. Pinckney Diary, p. 47.
32. Helm Collection.
33. ibid.
34. Ralston B. Lattimore, *Fort Pulaski*. (National Park Service, 1968).
35. Dickinson Diary, p. 115
36. ibid, p. 166. Murray, op. cit., p. 199, claimed that 220 officers were picked out and put on board the *Cannonicus* for the trip to Hilton Head Island. Dickinson stated that on Feb. 20, 102 sick Confederate soldiers captured at Savannah were brought into Fort Pulaski.
37. Gillmore to Halleck, Feb. 13, 1865, *Official Records*, Ser. 1, Vol. 47, Pt. 2, pp. 412-413.
38. Vessel File, War Records Division, National Archives. After a trial run from Philadelphia to Chester, John Flanagan wrote to Gen. M. S. Meigs, Quartermaster General, on July 24, 1863, that the vessel had "the most beautiful working engine I have ever seen," and offered to sell it to the U. S. Government for $115,000.
39. Dickinson Diary, p. 172.
40. Vessel File, War Records Division, National Archives, E 1403. The *Illinois*, built in 1851, was registered in the name of Marshall O. Roberts, a wealthy New York merchant. See the file for the sale of the ship to the government for $400,000, and when it was later offered for sale at public auction with other government-owned steamers, only one offer of $25,000 was made. President Lincoln originally ordered its purchase at $400,000.

41. Gillmore to Halleck, March 5, 1865, *Official Records*, Vol. XLVII, pp. 697-698.
42. On Dec. 26, 1904, Jastremski sent an account of his escape from the Federal authorities to J. Ogden Murray, who published it in *The Immortal 600*, pp. 223-228.
43. Helm Collection, translated by Patrick Darcy.
44. Jastremski Service Record.
45. John D. Winters, *The Civil War in Louisiana,* p. 423, mentions that furloughs and discharges were issued to Louisiana troops still remaining on May 20, but General Smith didn't sign the agreement of surrender until June 2 on a ship off the shore of Galveston, Texas.
46. Jastremski Service Record.
47. ibid.

Chapter 6—Proud Cavalier of Louisiana

1. Baton Rouge Mayors are Forgotten Men, by Charles East, *State Times,* Nov. 14, 1956.
2. Frederick Stuart Allen, *A Social and Economic History of Baton Rouge, 1850-1860,* p. 1, L. S. U. thesis, 1936.
3. Ernest Gueymard, Gueymard Notebook, *State-Times,* July 2, 1974, p. 18-A.
4. Interview with George Reymond, Fort Delaware, June 9, 1974.
5. Elks' Souvenir of Baton Rouge, pp. 90-91.
6. Joseph Larguier was the son of Isidore and Rosalie (nee Serret) Larguier. Isidore Larguier, according to SJO-11, Catholic Life Center, died Oct. 7, 1848, at the age of 74, and his wife, Rosalie, for whom Rosa Jastremski was probably named, in 1839 at the age of 50.
7. SJO, p. 99, Catholic Life Center.
8. SJO-19, p. 58.
9. In a copy of "Palmier Celeste," which Jastremski received from Mlle. M. E. R. in Baltimore, Md., on March 30, 1865, he listed the names of his children, the day and hour they were born. For Eugene Joseph, he wrote that he was born on Monday at 6:30 p. m., April 20, 1868; John Henry, August 7, 1869, Sunday, 2:30 p. m.; Estelle Marie, Dec. 16, 1871, Sunday, 6:30 p. m. Eugene, as he was called, spent practically his entire life in Baton Rouge, except when he went away to school or to serve as business manager of his father's newspapers in New Orleans and Shreveport and Baton Rouge. He was secretary in the state department of agriculture the last twenty years of his life. The affection of Eugene and Henry for each other was like that of Damon and Pythias.
10. Dr. Kratz to Jastremski, Feb. 10, 1868, and Jastremski to Callihan and Dubroca, Feb. 10, 1868. Copy of agreement, signed by James O. Fuqua, Wm. Reynaud, J. Warren Jones, Andrew J. Herron, and Thomas J. Buffington, Feb. 11, 1868, and their letter to James Cooper and David Callihan, Feb. 10, 1868, in Jastremski family papers, Helm Collection.

11. Jastremski was involved in another duel between Major E. A. Burke, editor of the New Orleans *Democrat,* and Major H. J. Hearsey, editor of *Daily States,* on Jan. 27, 1880. For details, see the *Daily States,* and *Daily Picayune* between January 25 and Feb. 1, 1880. Jastremski and Guy Carleton, a substitute, accompanied Major Hearsey in a carriage to a rendezvous on Metairie Ridge in New Orleans. After Jastremski and the other seconds selected a spot and chose the word upon which to fire, the two editors faced each other ten paces apart with loaded pistols which they had drawn, both being in the shade of a large oak tree, and each fired one shot without effect. The seconds met to see if either editor was ready to apologize for an editorial reflecting on Major Hearsey. The weapons were reloaded and the duellists again took their posts. The word being given they fired the second time, but only one report was heard. The result was the same as in the first instance. The seconds met again and agreed that Major Burke would not doubt the honor and bravery of Major Hearsey.
12. Louisiana Almanac and Fact Book, 1962, p. 46.
13. Baton Rouge *City Records,* Book C., May 18, 1868, quoted in Robert J. Aertker, *A Social History of Baton Rouge During the Civil War and Early Reconstruction,* p. 112, 115. LSU thesis, 1947.
14. Charles East, Baton Rouge Mayors are Forgotten Men, *State-Times,* Nov. 14-15, 1956.
15. In 1875, Jastremski organized the Baton Rouge Zouaves and served as its captain. His commission was signed by Gov. Francis T. Nicholls, April 27, 1877, and is on exhibit in the Memorial Room of the Captain Stanislaus Mlotkowski Brigade Society, Fort Delaware, by courtesy of Mrs. Sarah Jastremski Helm.
16. Report of Committees of the Senate of the U. S., 2nd Session, 44th Congress, 1876-77, p. 2103, hereinafter cited as Jastremski testimony.
17. *ibid.* p. 2097.
18. *ibid.* p. 2097.
19. *ibid.* p. 2098.
20. *ibid.* p. 2099.
21. *ibid.* p. 2103.
22. *ibid.* p. 2103.
23. Matlack to Jastremski, Nov. 6, 1898, Jastremski family papers, Helm Collection.
24. Minutes of special meeting of City Council, May 15, and citizens meeting, May 16, 1879, Joseph Larguier presiding, Baton Rouge, in Jastremski family papers, Helm Collection.
25. According to a newspaper clipping from the *Sugar Planter* (not dated) in Jastremski family papers, Helm Collection, several citizens of Baton Rouge, as Jastremski said, "seized me *ri et armis,* before I knew what they were about, and conducted me to the old billiard saloon of the Sumter House, where at a table magnificently covered with the best and daintiest in the land, they brought me to a halt." Major Andrew S. Herron, spokesman of the group, presented the "blushing, trembling and very much confused recepient with a magnificent gold watch and chain." The case was engraved. It had on one side a view of the State House

and on the other the initials, "L. J." The following inscription was on the inside of the case: "Presented to Gen. Leon Jastremski by his friends for his arduous and zealous efforts in the restoration of the State Capitol to Baton Rouge, May 14th 1881." The watch was bought from John Johnson, a Baton Rouge jeweler, and, in view of the curiosity of the public to see it, General Jastremski let the jeweler exhibit it in his store window for a few days.

26. Jastremski family papers, Helm Collection.
27. Ella Lonn, *Francis Redding Tillou Nicholls,* Dictionary of American Biography, Vol. VII, pp. 487-488.
28. Herman C. Nixon, *Louis Alfred Wiltz,* D. A. B., Vol. X, pp. 368-369; Fortier, Vol. 1, p. 262, 654-655.
29. Melvin J. White, *Samuel Douglas McEnery,* D. A. B., Vol. VI, p. 39; Fortier, Vol. 1, pp. 112-117.
30. Shreveport *Times,* June 28, 1893; Mrs. Sallie Land Jastremski Scrapbook, Helm Collection.
31. Undated clipping from Shreveport *Times* in Jastremski family papers, Helm Collection.
32. W. T. Dickinson Dalzell was born in the West Indies, on the island of St. Vincent, June 7, 1828, the son of an English sugar planter. He studied for the ministry in England and before the war, he moved to Houston, Texas. He entered the Confederate service and served as a chaplain of a Texas regiment. He was called to take charge of St. Mark's in July, 1866, and remained there until his death.
33. Obituary of Mrs. Sallie Land Jastremski, *State Times,* Nov. 1, 1920. The funeral of Mrs. Jastremski, who died Oct. 30, 1920, was held from the residence of Mr. and Mrs. Henry Jastremski in Roseland Terrace. Services were conducted by Dr. T. M. Hunter of the First Presbyterian Church and interment was made in Magnolia Cemetery, Baton Rouge, La., not with the remains of General Jastremski, who was buried in Old Catholic Cemetery on Main Street. She was responsible for the story-telling tombstone on his grave.
34. Elks' Souvenir of Baton Rouge, p. 90.
35. Louisiana Newspapers, 1794-1940, p. 19. The newspaper was later issued tri-weekly and Jastremski planned to convert it into a daily as soon as the capital was returned and the railroad completed to Baton Rouge.
36. Jastremski family papers, Reymond Collection.
37. On Feb. 5, 1881, General Jastremski, according to a receipt in the Jastremski family papers, Helm Collection, paid Mary Lane $7.50 for tuition of his daughter during two and a half months.
38. The commission, on loan from Mrs. Sarah Jastremski Helm, is on exhibit in the Memorial Room of the Captain Stanislaus Mlotkowski Memorial Brigade Society, Fort Delaware.
39. *ibid.*
40. Leon Jastremski was mentioned as a candidate for governor as early as 1882. He stepped aside for the incumbent governor, Samuel D. McEnery, and when Jastremski himself ran for governor in 1903, McEnery acted as chairman of the

committee for his Democratic opponent, Newton Blanchard. Late in 1882 the newspapers announced that he was one of the candidates to fill the vacancy caused by the death of Representative-elect Andrew S. Herron before the beginning of the 48th Congress, but Edward T. Lewis, a lawyer from Opelousas, was elected Feb. 15, 1883, to fill the vacancy. It is not known if Jastremski's name appeared on the ballot or he dropped out at the district nominating convention.

41. The members of the Printing Board consisted of John F. Pollock, New Orleans, Thomas Y. Aby, Quachita parish, Frank D. Chretien, New Orleans, Samuel M. Robertson, Baton Rouge, and William A. Seay, Shreveport.
42. Agreement of Jan. 4, 1882, in Jastremski family papers, Helm Collection, together with bids submitted to State Printing Board.
43. Copy of printing contract between Printing Board and Jastremski, Jan. 14, 1882, in Jastremski family papers, Helm Collection.
44. Agreement of March 21, 1888, in Jastremski family papers, Helm Collection.
45. Fortier, pp. 617-618.
46. Newspaper clipping, no date, Jastremski family papers, Helm Collection.
47. Fortier, pp. 563-564; The Organization of U. C. V., by Capt. Leon Jastremski, *Confederate Veteran,* Vol. XII, (1905), p. 425.
48. Louisiana Newspapers, 1794-1940, p. 175. A Union List of Louisiana Newspaper Files, prepared by Louisiana Historical Record Survey.
49. *Louisiana Review,* Jan. 1, 1890, p. 2. Howard-Tilton Library, New Orleans.
50. *ibid.,* Dec. 4, 1889, p. 2. For Jastremski's attitude on politics, see issue of August 6, 1890.
51. *ibid.*
52. Agreement is dated Nov. 14, 1893, and is in the Jastremski family papers, Helm Collection. Prior to the sale of the firm, Eugene Jastremski was business manager of *Louisiana Review,* 1893 New Orleans City Directory, p. 446.
53. Mrs. Jastremski's literary output was appraised in the *Daily States,* according to undated clipping in Jastremski family papers, Helm Collection.
54. *Louisiana Review,* July 9, 1890, p. 2. General Jastremski published lengthy accounts of meetings of the United Confederate Veterans.
55. For Mrs. Leon Jastremski's account, see *Louisiana Review,* Sept. 3, 1890, pp. 5-6. She wrote that she loved to "watch the sunset and see the god of day die like a dolphin, with changing lines of red, and purple, and gold, and each more lovely than the last."

Chapter 7—Consul In Callao

1. Henry J. Hearsey to Grover Cleveland, March 20, 1893. Jastremski Personal File, National Archives.
2. State Department Letters of Applications and Recommendations, 1893-97. National Archives.

3. *Minutes* of the City Council, Baton Rouge, La., March 23, 1893.
4. *Weekly Truth,* Baton Rouge, La., Dec. 2, 1893.
5. William Insco Buchanan, by Francis S. Philbrick. *Dictionary of American Biography,* edited by Allen Johnson and Dumas Malone (New York, 1929).
6. *New Orleans Picayune,* Nov. 3, 1893. It also states that "the appointment of Mr. Eustis to a first-class post, ambassador to France, operated as a serious obstacle to the nomination of a Louisianian for a position as minister." Through the efforts of U. S. Senator Donelson Caffery, the Callao consulship was given to Jastremski.
7. *Oaths of Office,* Record Group No. 59, and Jastremski to Edward M. Strobel, 3rd Assistant Secretary of State, Nov. 11, 1893, Consular Letters, Callao, Peru, 1898-1903, National Archives.
8. Jastremski to Strobel, Nov. 24, 1893, ibid; cabin passage card, Panama R. R. Co., Helm Collection.
9. Jastremski to Edwin F. Uhl, Assistant Secretary of State, Jan, 9. 1894; Jastremski to Senator D. Caffery, Feb. 28, 1893, and steamship ticket in Jastremski family papers.
10. Jastremski to Uhl, Jan. 19, 1894.
11. William Russell Grace, by Robert G. Albion. *Dictionary of American Biography,* edited by Allen Johnson & Dumas Malone, Vol. IV, p. 463 (New York, 1931); Peter Hevner, *A One sided History of Wm. R. Grace, the Pirate of Peru* (New York, 1888).
12. Jastremski to William W. Rockhill, Assistant Secretary of State, May 11, 1896.
13. Jastremski to Uhl, April 3, 1894.
14. Jastremski to Rockhill, Oct. 10, 1896.
15. Jastremski to Uhl, May 25, May 21, June 30, July 10, 16, 23, Sept. 3, Oct. 15, 1894; Jan. 5, 1895.
16. J. Phillips to Jastremski, May 21, 1894.
17. Jastremski to John Lee, April 25, 1894.
18. Jastremski to Uhl, Sept. 3, 1894.
19. Jastremski to Uhl, April 30, 1894.
20. Jastremski to Uhl, July 20, 1894.
21. Jastremski to Uhl, May 18, 1895.
22. R. J. Owens, *Peru,* pp. 42, 45, 49, 50 (New York, 1963).
23. Jastremski to Uhl, March 20, 1895.
24. *The Times-Democrat,* New Orleans, La., April 23, 1895.
25. Jastremski to Uhl, March 31, 1895.
26. *The Times-Democrat,* April 23, 1895.
27. ibid.
28. Jastremski to Captain H. D. Smith, March 29, 1895.
29. *The Daily Advocate,* Baton Rouge, La., May 14, 1895.

30. *The Times-Democrat,* May 15, 1895.
31. *Shreveport Times,* May 17, 1895.
32. Jastremski to Rockhill, July 18, 1896.
33. Jastremski to Rockhill, Feb. 18, 1897.
34. Jastremski to Rockhill, April 12, 1897.
35. Jastremski to Rockhill, telegram, April 12, 1897.
36. Jastremski to Rockhill, May 10, 1897.
37. Mrs. Sarah L. Helm, New Iberia, La., to Edward Pinkowski, Phila., May 6, 1974.
38. Jastremski to William R. Day, Assistant Secretary of State, July 3, 1897.
39. Caffery to Jastremski, April 23, 1894.

Chapter 8—The Last Campaign

1. *The Daily State,* Baton Rouge, La., Nov. 29, 1907.
2. *New Orleans Picayune,* Feb. 24, 1898. Leon Jastremski, *Advantages of New Orleans and Louisiana for Intercourse with South America* (Baton Rouge, 1898).
3. Shreveport (La.) *City Directory,* 1899, pp. 145, 169, 95, 110, 192.
4. *Baton Rouge City Directory,* 1905-06, p. 163.
5. *The Daily State,* Nov. 29, 1907.
6. *Biographical Directory of the American Congress.*
7. *The Daily State,* Nov. 29, 1907.
8. ibid.
9. *Louisiana Newspapers,* 1794-1940. (Louisiana Historical Record Survey, 1941).
10. *Baton Rouge City Directory,* 1906, p. 35.
11. *Conveyance Record,* Vol. 45, p. 465. Court House, Baton Rouge, La.
12. *Baton Rouge City Directory,* 1906, p. 209.
13. Alcee Fortier, *History of Louisiana,* vol. 3, p. 223.
14. *Baptism Register,* p. 328, St. Joseph's Cathedral, Baton Rouge, La.
15. *Memoirs of Louisiana,* Vol. 1, p. 493.
16. Significant Dates and Facts Pertaining to the family of William P. and Mrs. Rosa Jastremski Reymond, mss., George H. Reymond, Baton Rouge, La.
    Ernestine Marie Jastremski never married. In addition to teaching at the Deaf and Dumb Institute, she taught at Jacksonville, Illinois, and Randolph-Macon Woman's College, Lynchburg, Va., from which she retired. She died March 21, 1931.
17. ibid. Rose Henrietta (nee Jastremski) Reymond lived her entire life in Baton Rouge. She died March 15, 1945, and her husband died March 29, 1937. Both were buried side by side in Roselawn Cemetery, Baton Rouge.
18. ibid. John Joseph Reymond married Bertha Blanchard August 1, 1926. He obtained a Bachelor of Science degree in Sugar Chemistry from L. S. U.

19. William P. Reymond, Jr., graduated in Civil Engineering from L. S. U. Lieutenant, World War I, married Celeste Adler September 27, 1924, and they had one son, William Gene, born October 19, 1925. William Phillips Reymond died May 18, 1971.
20. George H. Reymond graduated from L. S. U. in Agriculture. Married Laura Redden September 19, 1935, and they had one son, Robert, born May, 1942, died March 28, 1960.
21. James B. Reymond graduated from L. S. U. in Civil Engineering. Married Marcia Hammon Oct. 5, 1960, died Nov. 16, 1973, without issue.
22. Mary Leontine Reymond attended St. Joseph's Convent and Dominican College, New Orleans, graduated from American College of Physical Education in Chicago and L. S. U. Married Stephen A. Theard October 18, 1925, and he died Sept. 13, 1961.
23. Leon Jastremski Reymond graduated from L. S. U. in Commerce. Married Florence Vincent, of New Orleans, Feb. 12, 1942, and they had three children, Leon Jastremski, born Nov. 26, 1942, Mary Ann and Linda. He died November 26, 1965.
24. *Memoirs of Louisiana,* Vol. 1, p. 493.
25. Dr. Vincent Jastremski died in Montegut, La., during influenza epidemic in October, 1918. He had no children. His mother, Leontine Keays Jastremski, died October 18, 1914, at his home in Montegut and was buried beside her husband in the Old Catholic Cemetery, Baton Rouge, La., in the same family plot as General Jastremski. She was born May 28, 1842, in Iberville Parish, La.
26. *The Daily State,* Nov. 29, 1907.
27. *ibid.*
28. ibid.
29. ibid.
30. ibid.
31. ibid.
32. ibid.
33. *Abbeville Meridional,* Dec. 7, 1907, on which Leon Jastremski began his career in 1856, said, "The noble spirit of Leon Jastremski left its earthly tenement and the grand old man was gathered to his fathers."
34. *The Daily State,* Nov. 29, 1907.
35. George H. Reymond to Pinkowski, June 8, 1971.

INDEX

(Appendices and Bibliographical Notes not included)

Abbeville, La., 10, 12, 15, 29, 32-36, 80, 84
Abbeville Meridional, 12, 15, 34, 36
Adams, Lt. Dick, 71
Admiral, U. S. gunboat, 66
Ahl, Capt. George, 59
Alans, 24
Alexandria, La., 84
Allen, Lt. Cicero M., 75-77, 79
Alliance, U. S. ship, 101
Anderson, Lt. Col. Smith W., 81
Andersonville, Ga., 51
Amedee, Joyce, 12
American Impressions, 30-31
American Polonia Reporter, 16
Andes Mountains, Peru, 101
Archacki, Henry, 13, 15-16
Argentina, 99
Army of Northern Virginia, 9, 39-62, 79
Army of the Potomac, 39, 44, 47
Ashland, steamer, 74-75
Ashton, Major James H., 92
Ashton, Mrs. Sallie Land, 92
Atlanta, Ga., 70
Auguste, childhood companion, 28

Babiarz, Adela, 20
Babiarz, John, 20
Babiarz, Raymond, 21
Baczkowski, Julia, 20
Bailey, Mrs. Kate C., 115
Baker, Thomas J., Jr., 12
Baltimore, Md., 79
Barrie, Robert, 107-108
Baton Rouge, La., 10, 12, 15, 21, 31-32, 36, 80-81, 83-94, 97, 99, 112, 117-123
Battery Gregg, 69-70
Baxter, William, 65-67
Beaufort, S. C., 67
Becinski, B., 31
Belle Plaine, Va., 53
Bertrand, Octave, 33
Bertrand, Vincent, 33
Berryville, 44
Bieganski, Edward, 32
Bienvenu, Ralph R., 12
Blaine, James G., 95
Blair, Albert, 13
Blanchard, Newton C., 116-117, 119, 122
Bloody Angle of Spottsylvania, 47, 53-54, 62
Blozis, Tillie, 20
Bodin, Rev. Msgr. George A., 12
Bolivia, 103
Boissier, Mrs. V., 33
Bradley, James, 36
Braux, Dame Celeste, 29
Brockenbrough, Eleanor S., 12

Brown, Col. P. P., 72-73
Brown, John M., 65
Bryan, Benjamin F., 83
Buchanan, Wm. I., 99-100
Buenos Aires, 99-100
Buffington, Dr. Thomas J., 86
Bull Run, 45
Bunyan, John, 51
Burton, Major Henry S., 52
Butler, General Ben, 40
Bynum, Wade H., 121

Caceres, Gen. Andres, 111-112
Caffery, Senator Donelson, 10, 100-101, 114
Cairo, Illinois, 80
Callahan, Mrs. Harriet, 12
Callihan, David M., 86
Callao, Peru, 9, 99-114
Camp Marigny, Va., 38
Camp Squatley, Va., 38
Canby, Gen. E. R. S., 81
Cape Hatteras, 66, 75
Cape Romain, 67
Capitolian-Advocate, 115, 118
Carbonne, France, 28
Carlisle, Pa., 44
Castres, Vincent, 28
Catholic Life Center, Baton Rouge, 12
Chambersburg, Pa., 44-45
Chancellorsville, Va., 56-59
Chantilly, Va., 42
Charleston, S. C., 59, 62-63, 67-70, 72, 78
Chattanooga, Tenn., 97-98
Chiclayo, Peru, 105
Chourre, 28
Cincinnati, Ohio, 96
City Hotel, Shreveport, 115
Cleveland, Grover, 95, 99-100, 112, 114
Clover, election official, 89
Cole, W., 108, 110
Coleman, Mrs. Marion Moore, 30
Colon, Panama, 100
Columbus, Ohio, 96
Commodore Perry, U. S. revenue steamer, 111
Concordia Sentinel, 97
Conrad, Joseph, 22
Constantine, viceroy of Poland, 25
Constitutional convention, 91-92, 121
Cooper, Capt. James, 85-86
Corwalski, M., 32
Corwin, Joseph, 31
Council of Polish Societies and Clubs in Del., 17-18
Craig, Ernest D., 100
Crescent, prison ship, 63, 65-69, 77

Cromwell, Oliver, 11
Crouchet, Michel, 32
Culpeper, Va., 41, 46
Culp's Hill, 46
Cupery, Martin, 12
Cuzco, Peru, 110-111
Czar Alexander I, 25
Czar Nicholas, 25
Czarnowski, Oscar, 32
Czar Paul I, 25

Dabrowski, Edmund, 20
Dabrowski, Joe, 19
Daily Advocate, 94-95, 112
Daily Capitolian-Advocate, 94-95, 97
Daily States, 101, 112-113, 120, 122
Dalzell, Rev. Dr. Wm. T. D., 92
Dam No. 1, 39
Darcy, Patrick, 12
Davis, Jefferson, 9, 79
Day, William R., 114
Delacroix, Rev. C., 85
Delaware City, Del., 18
Delaware River, 65
Democrats, 87-89, 91, 99
de Pointes, Ernestine Marguerite, 26
De Priest, Capt. Emmett E., 75-77
Derveloy, Mrs. Lillian Steen, 12
Dick, a slave, 29
Dickey, Wm. B., 89-90
Dillingham, Mary E. (Mrs. Thomas T. Land), 91
Dillon, Mariah (Mrs. Kajetan Kowalewski), 30
Dubroca, Col. Ed., 86
Duval, Dr. Cleburne A., 118
Duval, Julia (Easton), 118
Duval, Gwinette (Mrs. Leon Jastremski), 118-119

Easton, Julia, 118
Eaton, Capt. Wm. B., 67
Edinburg, 44
Elam, James E., 87
English settlers in Peru, 113
English vessels, 104
Evansville, Ind., 79-80
Ewell, Gen. Eugene S., 44, 46-47
Eyre, John, 105

Falkowski, Joseph, 18
Farragut, Admiral David G., 83
Fielding, Henry, 23
Fifth Maryland Infantry, 53
Fifty-fourth Massachusetts Infantry, 68-72, 78
Floyd, Del, 13
Follot, Rev. Francis C., 33
Folly Island, S. C., 71
Forbes, Charles, 108

Fort Delaware, 9, 15-22, 41, 47, 49-63, 65, 75-77, 79
Fort Delaware Society, 17
Fort Moultrie, 70
Fort Pulaski, Ga., 72-75, 78
Fortress Monroe, Va., 53, 78
Fort Sumter, 35-36, 70
Fort Wagner, 69-70
Fort Warren, 52
Foster, Major Gen. J. G., 59-60, 67, 70, 72, 74, 78
Foster, Murphy J., 95-96
Fourteenth Louisiana Infantry, 38
France, 10, 26
Frank, William P., 17
Franklin, La., 80-81
Frederick, Md., 42
Fredericksburg, 44, 116
Free Market Hall, Baton Rouge, 88
French immigrants, 28-30, 32-33
Fuqua, Col. J. O., 84

Garbowski, Edward, 20
Garig, William, 92, 95
Garig-Wilson Co., 117
Gastal, Francois, 34
German vessels, 104
Gettysburg, Pa., 45-47, 56, 116
Gibson, Captain Augustus A., 50-52
Gillmore, Major Gen. Q. A., 74
Gordon, Gen. John B., 97
Gorlinski, Joseph N., 31-32
Gorlinski, Valentina, 31
Goslinski, Gustavus, 32
Grace, Michael P., 103-104
Grace, William R., 102-104, 112
Grand Army of the Republic, 96
Grant, Peter, 108
Grant, Gen. Ulysses S., 46-47, 70, 79
Grenada, Miss., 80
Guegnon, Eugene I., 34, 36
Guegnon, Valerie, 34
Gueydan, La., 34
Gueydan, Jean Pierre, 33-34
Gueymard, Ernest, 12

Halleck, Major Gen. Henry W., 74
Hallowell, Col. E. N., 71
Hancock, Gen. W. S., 47, 52
Handy, Rev. Isaac W. K., 53, 55, 60, 63
Harper's Ferry, 42-43
Harrison, G. W., 107
Havana, Cuba, 79, 112
Hayes, Rutherford B., 87-90
Heard, Gov. William Wright, 116
Hearsey, Major H. James, 99, 101-102
Helm, Sarah Land Jastremski, 11, 26, 30
Heslop, J., 108
Hevner, Peter, 103
Hilton Head, S. C., 74

INDEX 169

Historical Society of Pa., 12
Hoffman, Col. Wm., 51, 54
Holloway, Frances, 117
Hooker, Gen. Joseph, 44
Houma, La., 118-119
Hugo, Victor, 38

Independence Fire Co., No. 2, Baton Rouge, 87
In De Prison Ob Fort Delaware, 60-61
Illinois, 75-77, 79
Immortal 600, 59-60, 62-63, 65-81

Jackson, Andrew, 38
Jackson, Major Andrew, 85-86
Jackson, Laura, 86
Jackson, Gen. "Stonewall," 35, 41-45, 52
Jamestown Poles, 21
Jardremsky, 37
Jasdremski, 37
Jastermiskie, 37
Jastramski, 37
Jastraupski, 37
Jastremski, Ernestine, 56-57, 63, 118
Jastremski, Estelle Marie, 86, 90-93, 117
Jastremski, Eugene Joseph, 86, 97, 114-117, 120-121
Jastremski, Frances (Mrs. Henry), 117, 121
Jastremski, Gwinette, 118-119
Jastremski, John Duval, 119
Jastremski, John Henry, 86, 97, 114, 116-117, 119-121
Jastremski, John (Jean) Vincent, 28-29, 33-34, 36, 38, 53-55, 57, 62-63, 69-70, 73-79, 83-84, 87, 101, 117-118
Jastremski, Julia (Mrs. Patrick L. Higgins), 119
Jastremski, Leon, letter to President Wm. McKinley, 9-10; parents, 10, 23-24, 26; birth and childhood, 10, 28-29; employment, 10, 15, 36, 84-85; military service, 9, 15, 35-48, 52, 56, 59; prisoner of war, 47-49; parole, 80-81, 84; marriages, 85, 92; children, 11, 86, 92-94; duel, 86; voting, 11, 87; membership in Ku Klux Klan, 87; mayor of Baton Rouge, 15, 187-92; presidential elections, 10, 87-89, 95; newspaper editor, 92-97; diplomatic career, 99-114; candidacy for governor, 116-120; death, 120
Jastremski, Leon (grandnephew), 119
Jastremski, Leon Henry, 118-119
Jastremski, Leontine, 79, 86, 117-118
Jastremski, Margaret, 119
Jastremski, Marguerite, 32-34
Jastremski, Rosa, 85-86, 90
Jastremski, Rosa Henrietta, 118, 123
Jastremski, Sallie Land, 97-98, 101-102, 113, 115, 120

Jastremski, Sarah Land, 117, 121
Jastremski, Stanwood Duval, 119
Jastremski, Therese, 26
Jastremski, Dr. Vincent, 24-34, 37
Jastremski, Vincent (grandnephew), 119
Jastrzebski, Agnes, 23
    Basil, 23
    Benedict, 23
    Dominick, 23
    John, 23
    Joseph, 23
    Michael, 23, 24
    Nicholas, 23
    Stephen, 23
    Thomas, 23
Jastrzembski, Blazej, 27
    Joseph, 28
    Justinian, 26-28
    Louis, 27
    Mrs., 26-28
Jefferson, Thomas, 118
Johnson, Lt., 112
Johnson, President Andrew, 86
Johnston, Gen. Edward, 47
Jonkiert, Casimir, 20
Jones, Major Gen. Sam, 59-60
Jones, Col. T. Sambola, 94-95, 115

Kamieniec, 24
Kamienietz Podolski, 25-26
Karge, Col. Joseph, 20
Kattie, Moreen, 12
Keays, Mrs. Henrietta, 55-57, 63, 79-80, 83, 85
Keays, Henry, 55
Keays, Leontine (Mrs. John Jastremski), 33, 79, 83, 85, 117
Keays, Oliver, 55, 57
Kilczewski, Charles, 12, 19, 20, 21
Kilczewski, Helen, 12, 18-20
King John Casimir, 23
Klaczkiewicz, Czeslawa, 18
Klosy (Ears of Grain), 30
Knights of Pythias, 96
Knights of the White Camelia, 87
Kolski, Anna, 28
Kopec, Ludwig, 18
Kosciuszko, Gen. Thaddeus, 16, 21, 26, 72
Kowalewski, Dr. Kajetan, 30
Kowalewski, Joanne, 19-20
Kowalewski, John, 19, 21
Kowalewski, Josephine, 19
Kowalewski, Vincent J., 17-19
Kowalski, A., 31
Kozlowski, Mr. & Mrs. Chester T., 21
Kozinski, Emilie, 21
Kratz, Dr. O., 86
Ku Klux Klan, 87
Kucharska, Carolyn, 20
Kurczyn, N. J. W., 32

Lafayette, La., 12, 32
L'Amite Democrat, 36
Land, Charles, 91
Land, John, 91
Land, Sallie, 92
Land, Sarah, 91
Land, Thomas T., 91-92
Lane, Mary, 93
la Noue, Eugene, 85
La Paz, Bolivia, 103
La Punta, Peru, 101
Larguier, Elisa, 85
Larguier, Joseph, 85, 87
Larguier, Rosa (Adelaide Rose), 85-86
Latham, Capt. Daniel D., 65-67, 69
Lawryntowicz, Dr. Francis, 31
Lege, Alexander, 34
Leski, Frank J., 18
Lee, John, 106-109
Lee, Gen. Robert E., 35, 39-40, 42-47, 62, 79-80
Lelvy, Peter, 11
LeSueur, Sadie Bird, 93-94
LeSueur, William A., 92-94
Liberty, Miss., 36
Library of Congress, 12
Lima, Peru, 100-101, 103, 105, 109, 111-114
L'Imitation de Jesus Christ, 85
Lincoln, President Abraham, 10, 43-44, 47, 74
Lingren, John, 108
Lipinski, C., 32
Lis, Edward, 22
Liszkiewicz, Anthony, 20
Logical Point, The, 102
Longstreet, James, 46
Lookout Mountain, Tenn., 98
Louisiana, 10-12, 15-16, 28-35, 37, 99-100, 116, 120
Louisiana Capitolian, 92-94
Louisiana Deaf and Dumb Institute, 116, 118
Louisiana Experiment Station, 111
Louisiana National Guard, 9
Louisiana Review, 97
Louisiana State Printing Board, 94
Louisiana State University, 94, 118
Louisiana Swamp Rifles, 37
Louis Philippe, king of France, 26, 28
Lytle, Andrew D., 85

Maczynski, Janina (Jennie), 21
Maczynski, Walter, 21
Madison, 44
Magdycz, Joanne (Kowalewski), 19-20
Magruder, Gen. John B., 37-39
Maine, U. S. battleship, 9
Make One More Gun for Me! a poem, 9
Malvern Hill, Va., 39-40, 49, 51-52

Marigny, Col. Mandeville de, 37
Martinez, Nina, 118
Martinsburg, 43
Maryland, 42, 44
Matlack, Thomas E., 90
Maryland, My Maryland, 35, 42
McBride, William S., 105-107, 114
McClellan, Major Gen. George B., 39-40, 43
McEnery, Samuel D., 90-91, 95, 114
McGrath, John, 85, 99
McKenzie, A., 107
McKenzie, James A., 100-101, 103, 105, 111-114
McKinley, William, 114-115
Meade, Gen. George G., 45-46
Medford, Maine, 106
Megret, Abbe A. D., 32
Memphis, Tenn., 80
Meridian, Miss., 80
Methodists, 113-114
Mioton, E. T., 78
Mississippi River, 84, 118
Mlotkowski, Capt. Stanislaus, 17, 20-21, 50-51, 54-55
Mlotkowski, Captain Stanislaus Memorial Brigade Society, 13, 16, 20-22
Mollendo, Peru, 105-109
Monroe, President James, 84
Montegut, La., 119
Mooney, John, 107
Moonlight, ex-Gov. of Dakota, 103
Montpellier, France, 26
Morris House, Shreveport, 115
Morris Island, S. C., 9, 59-60, 67-73, 78
Mouton, Alexander, 28-29, 35
Mouton, Rev. Msgr. Richard von Phul, 12
Murphy, Capt. J. C., 81
Museum of the Confederacy, Richmond, 12
Musick, Michael P., 13

National Archives, 12-13
National Press Association, 96
Negro slaves, 29-31, 38-39
Negro troops, 68-72, 78, 89
Negro voters, 87-88
New Orleans, La., 9, 30, 32-33, 36-37, 40, 91-92, 95-99, 110, 114-116
New Orleans Bee, 97
New Orleans Daily States, 99
Newburyport, Mass., 113
New York, 76-77, 79, 100, 104
Nicholls, Francis, 89-91, 95-96
Nigger of the Narcissus, The, 22
Ninety-third U. S. Colored Infantry, 80-81
North, Evelyne, 21
North, Sydney D., 21
Nowak, Florence, 21

Oladowski, Hypolite, 31
One hundred fifty-seventh New York Infantry, 72

INDEX

Opelousa, La., 84
Orleans Blues, 43
Oroya, Peru, 101
Otis, Olive, nom de plume of Mrs. Sallie Jastremski, 97
Ox Hill (Chantilly), Va., 42

Pacific Ocean, 101
Pacific Steam Navigation Co., 113
Packard, Stephen B., 89
Paita, Peru, 105
Palczewski, Irene, 21
Palczewski, Ted, 21
Panama, 100
Panama Canal, 110
Paruszewski, Charles, 20
Paruszewski, Jean, 20
Pawlikowski, Ben, 20
Pea Patch Island, 16, 49-63
Pennsylvania Artillery, 20
People, The, 117
Perkins, Capt. Thomas F., 75-76
Phillips, J., 106-107
Pierola, Nicolas de, 111
Pilgrim's Progress, 51
Pilitowski, August, 32
Pinckney, Capt. Thomas, 58-59
Pinkowski, Connie, 12
Pisgah Church, Va., 47
Pitkin, John R. G., 99
Piura, Peru, 105
Pizarro, 110
Plaquemine, La., 33, 120
Plaza de Acho, Peru, 110
Plitt, Frank, 21
Podolia, 23-24
Point Lookout, Md., 53
Point of Rocks, Md., 79
Poland, 23-29
Polish American Historical Association, 15
Polish press, 15, 17
Polish settlers, 30-32, 72
Polish War Mothers, 18
Pope, Gen. John, 41-42, 52
Porter, Gov. of Tenn., 103
Port Royal, S. C., 67
Potomac River, 53
Prachenski, Rev. Joseph, 31-32
Prentiss, Capt. James H., 66-67
Pulaski, Gen. Casimir, 16, 21, 72

Queenstown, Ireland, 103

Raczynski, Gen. John, 72
Radzinski, Dr. Louis D., 72
Randall, James Ryder, 35
Randolph, Tenn., 80
Rapidan River, Va., 46
Reimer, Mrs. Josephine, 21
Republicans, 87-90, 114

Reymond, D. F., 118
  Etta, 118
  George Hebb, 12, 21-22, 118
  Henrietta, 118
  James Bernard, 118
  John Joseph, 118
  Laura, 12, 21
  Leon Jastremski, 118
  Mary Leontine, 118
  William Phillips, 118
  William Phillips, Jr., 118
Reynaud, Dr. Louis F., 120-121
Richmond, Va., 12, 37-39, 46, 79
Ritchie, John, 71
Robertson, Samuel M., 99
Rockhill, Wm. W., 104-105, 113-114
Rosiak, Adam, 20
Rybaltowski family, 21
Rybicki, Theodore, 31

St. John the Evangelist R. C. Church, Plaquemine, 33
St. Marie Madeleine Church, Abbeville, 32
St. Mark's Episcopal Church, Shreveport, 92
St. Joseph's Convent, Baton Rouge, 93
St. Joseph's R. C. Church, Baton Rouge, 85, 123
St. Stanislaus College, Bay St. Louis, 119
St. Stanislaus, Wilmington, Del., 19
St. Vincent's Young Ladies Academy, Cape Girardeau, Missouri, 118
Salva, steamer, 53
Sanders, Jared Y., 119-120
Sanders, Major John, 49-50
San Francisco, 106
Sanitary Commission, 45
San Lorenzo Island, Peru, 103
Sarmatians, 24
Savannah, Ga., 72
Savoy, Mrs. Blanche (Mrs. Vincent Jastremski), 119
Schoepf, Gen. Albin F., 20, 53-55, 59
Schoonmaker, S. H. B., 87
Schtcherbowietz, 25-28
Second Louisiana Brigade, 43
Sedgwick, Gen. John, 47
Seventh Brigade, 38-39
Seven Days' Battles, 39
Sharpsburg (Antietam), 43, 116
Shenandoah Valley, 42, 44
Sherman, Gen. Wm. T., 74, 75
Shippensburg, Pa., 44
Shreveport, La., 84, 91-92, 99, 115
Shreveport Outlook, 115-116
Shreveport Times, 113
Sixty-ninth New York Infantry, 40-41
Skomorucha, Edward, 18
Skorupski, Ignatius, 32
Smith, Capt. H. D., 112
Smith, Gen. E. Kirby, 80-81

Smulski, Francis, 21
Sobieski, John (King John III), 23-24
Sobocinski, Stanley, 20-22
Sobocinski, Zenon, 20
Soulan, France, 28
Spangler, Rev. J. M., 113
Spanish-American War, 9
Spottsylvania, Va., 9, 47, 52-54, 56, 62
S. S. *Voy*, steamship, 100
Stanton, Secy. of War Edwin, 51
Stan, Walt, 20
Staszczak, Walter, 12, 20-21
Steckiewicz, Francis, 31
Steen, Mr. & Mrs. Albert, 12
Stepnowski, Ann, 20
Stepnowski, Blanche, 20
Stepnowski, Bronislawa, 18
Stewart, James, 13
Stow, George W., 66
Strasburg, 44
Strawenski, 37
Strzalkowski, Joseph, 18
Sulakowski, Col. Valery, 38
Sulimirski, Dr. Tadeusz, 24
Swan, steamer, 53
Szymanski, Ignatius, 31-32

Taylor, Gen. Richard B., 80
Taylor, Gen. Zachary, 49
Templar, American bark, 106-110
Tenth La. Infantry, 9, 37-38, 40-41, 46-48, 52-53, 94
Terepka, Mr. & Mrs. Alex, 21
Theocritus, 22
Thomas, Dana Lee and Henry, 43
Thornton Gap, 44
Tice, Julianna Kilczewski, 21
Tilden, Samuel J., 87, 89
Tomczyk, Mr. & Mrs. Walter, 21
Trujillo, Peru, 105
Tumbes, Peru, 105
Turochy, Aniela, 20
Twelfth U. S. Regulars, 41

Uhl, Edwin F., 107, 110-111
Ukraine, 30

Uminski, Sigmund, 15-16
United Confederate Veterans, 96-98
U. S. Naval Academy, 118
University of Virginia, 91

Vancouver, 106-107
Vermilion parish, 32-35
Vermilionville (Lafayette), La., 10, 29, 32, 33, 35

Waggaman, Col. Eugene, 37-41, 51-52
Waggaman, George A., 38
Walker, James, 13
Walter, William, 86
Warsaw, 25
Washington Fire Co., Baton Rouge, 85, 87
Weekly Truth, Baton Rouge, 99
Wells, Gov. J. Madison, 87
Wheelwright, Capt. Wm., 113
White's Ford, Md., 42
Wiadomosci, 17
Wilderness, 116
William, a mulatto boy, 29
Williams, Ramon, 112
Williamsburg, Va., 39
Wilmington, Del., 17-19
Wilson, W. Emerson, 12, 17-18
Wiltz, Gov. Louis A., 91, 94-95
Winchester, 44
Wing, William, 66
Wisowaty, Walter, 18
Witt, Anthony, 20
Wolski, Kalikst, 30-31
Woodward, W. E., 47
Wrotnowski, Arthur, 31
    Stanislaus, 31
    Stanislaus A., 31
    Valentina, 31
Wysocki, Piotr, 25, 30

Yasik, John, 20
Yatkowski, Ben. S., Sr., 21
Yorktown, 9

Zabrda, P., 28